Hey Carter—
I'm not Mark Hurd)
😊
but...
TAB 6/07

PAPER PROBLEMS

TAKING CONTROL OF YOUR DISTRIBUTED OFFICE OUTPUT ENVIRONMENT

VOLUME I: GENERAL OFFICE PRINT, COPY AND FAX

PAPER PROBLEMS

VOLUME I: GENERAL OFFICE PRINT, COPY AND FAX

TAB EDWARDS

A TAB REPORT BOOK

PUBLISHED BY OXFORD HILL PRESS

Philadelphia   New York   Chicago   Toronto

OXFORD HILL PRESS

A Division of *The Oxford Hill Consulting Group*

ISBN 0-9700891-1-2; (paper back)

This publication is designed to provide authoritative information in regards to the subject matter covered. It is sold with the understanding that the publisher is not engaged in rendering legal, accounting, or other professional services. If legal advice or other expert assistance is required, the services of a competent professional person should be sought.

—From a declaration of principles jointly adopted by a committee of the American Bar Association and a committee of publishers.

Oxford Hill Press books are available at special quantity discounts to use as premiums and sales promotions, or for use in corporate training programs. For more information, please visit the website: www.oxfordhill.com or www.oxfordhillpress.com.

Designed by Joshua Black of Blackeyesoup.com
Philadelphia, PA.

CONTENTS

CONTENTS (CONTINUED)

	Chapter		Page

"The information industry today is like a huge electronic piñata, composed of a thin paper crust surrounding an electronic core. The growing paper crust is most noticeable, but the hidden electronic core that produces the crust is far larger — and growing more rapidly. The result is that we are becoming paperless, but we hardly notice at all."

PAUL SAFFO, A TECHNOLOGY FORECASTER AT THE INSTITUTE FOR THE FUTURE

PREFACE

TIME FLIES. THOUGH IT'S BEEN NEARLY 10-YEARS since I first had a conversation with a customer about the value of performing an assessment of their distributed office output environment — print, copy, and fax — it seems as though it has only been a few months. How things have changed.

Attitudes have changed. There was a time when the hardcopy devices (priters, copiers, fax machines and scanners) were considered the step-child of the IT infrastructure; no one really paid too much attention to them. The prevailing wisdom was that printers weren't a big deal because they were relatively inexpensive to purchase and they were pretty reliable. So not many IT managers focused on this area when looking for opportunities to improve IT service levels or opportunities to reduce costs. Today, it is quite different.

Over the past ten years, IT managers have nearly exhausted all other opportunities for cost-cutting (including the data center, the desktop, the distributed server farm, etc.), so, almost out of desperation, they began looking at the print, copy and fax environments. To their surprise, this sector was rife with opportunities to cut costs and provide other efficiencies. Maybe it was all spurred on by that old, infamous statistic that was making the rounds back in the late '90s: "Companies on average spend

$1,200 per-year-per-employee on print, copy and fax." This number raised the eyebrows of many a CIO who suddenly began to conceptualize the opportunity for improvement if the company could somehow reduce these costs.

Everyone wanted to know what the potential for cost savings was, but that meant they must first understand how much they were spending.

Right about this time, consultants were offering up the idea of an assessment service through which companies could, indeed, determine how much they were spending on print, copy and fax, and at the same time, identify some of the other problems associated with the hardcopy environment. And thus, the floodgates were opened.

Methodologies have changed. I recall the first office output assessment I performed nearly 10 years ago. It involved the use of tracking software, copy-tracking devices, and all sorts of other things that I think about today and it makes me chuckle.

After a year of that complexity, I believed there was a better way to perform the data gathering portion of an office output study. So, I crafted a methodology that I believed customers would agree made sense, and that would yield more accurate results more quickly; I think it worked. And a few months later, I found myself applying this new method when I had to perform an assessment of a Fortune 100 company. This assessment involved 5,000 users and 23 buildings (not floors, but buildings!). Performing this massive assessment would not have been possible using the old method, so I used it debut my new approach; it worked! Not only that, but I learned more about the world of printers, copiers and fax machines during that one assessment than I had in all of the previous assessments I had performed to that date.

Through this book, I hope to share with you the value of my experiences over the years in hope that you will find a morsel of information that will help you in your office output improvement endeavors. Will you agree with everything I write herein? Maybe not. But I'm sure you'll find it intriguing nonetheless.

PART ONE

THE SITUATION

chapter one

WHY SO MUCH PAPER?

PCs AND TVs AND WEB, OH MY!

Come with me for a minute... On a typical Sunday morning, Bob West — your typical American — wakes up to begin his final day of "freedom" before returning to work on Monday morning. He goes into his kitchen and turns on the 21-inch television to watch the news while he prepares a cup of coffee. As he sips his coffee, he simultaneously reads the newspaper and semi-watches/listens to the TV news.

Bob's full attention is suddenly commanded by a shocking story on television, and he wants to get a better view. He runs into the family room to view this breaking news story on his big-screen plasma TV only to find his 2.5 kids watching cartoons there. He then rushes to the living room and discovers that his wife is watching a movie on the family's 42-inch set. Undaunted, he races up to the bedroom, turns on the 27-inch television and watches the remainder of the news program. But the Morning News doesn't provide Bob with the level of detail he wants about the news story. So he goes to the den to use one of the family's personal computers to access the Internet where he can search news sites for additional information about the breaking story.

When he enters the den, his son is playing video games (probably *World of Warcraft*) on the computer. So, Bob takes a detour to his home office, logs on to his office PC, and finds additional coverage of this breaking news story. Bob thinks this news so incredible that he shares it electronically — via e-mail and his cell phone — with his closest friends.

The next morning when Bob arrives at the corporate office, he logs-on to his e-mail and notices that other people have sent *him* messages about that breaking news story. He checks his cell phone and there, too, are messages received from his colleagues about the breaking news story. The story is suddenly the talk of the office. Many people print copies of the news story so that they can read it better, some print it so that they can read it later, some print it to share with others, and some print it for posterity sake (they don't really trust electronic storage yet). The result: *the exponential growth and sharing of information.*

EXPONENTIAL INFORMATION GROWTH

This story illustrates the way typical household consumer electronic devices can play a part in the way information is exponentially created, shared, and how it ultimately finds its way from the household to the business office.

Before I continue, what exactly is "information"? *Information* is defined as a collection of facts or data; communication of knowledge. A main tenet of this and other definitions of *information* is that these data, facts and knowledge must be communicated (i.e. spread).

There is a direct correlation between the number of consumer electronic devices in the household (including television sets, digital video recorders, radios, personal computers with Internet access, cellular phones & Personal Digital Assistants, portable music & video devices, and telephones), and the amount of information that is created and ultimately finds its way to the business office. In the United States, the number of said electronic devices and technologies has steadily increased over the last several years, as has our usage of these devices. According to the A.C. Nielsen Company, 99% of households have at least one television set; the number of TV sets in the average household is 2.24; 66% of U.S. homes have 3 or more TV sets; and the total average time a household watched television during the 2005-2006 television year was 8 hours and 14 minutes per day.

Nearly 66% of US households own PCs, and, the average number of PCs per PC-owning household is 1.5 (IDC). According to Pew Internet, the percentage of Americans who use the Internet has increased from 66% in January 2005 to 73%. (And according to support.com, 65% of US consumers are spending more time with a computer than with their significant other). And when you consider that about 75% of households have at least one cellular phone and at least two land-line phones, it becomes easier to see how the growth in information occurs exponentially; the exponential growth in the number of consumer electronics in U.S. households contributes to the generation and receipt of information and its exponential growth.

Consider that in 17th century England, communication with others was less frequent than it is today and there were no home consumer electronics (conduits of information) to speak of. According to *Information Anxiety*, the amount of information contained in a single edition of a daily newspaper today is more information than a person growing up in 17th century England will have seen in an entire lifetime!

NETWORKED PERSONAL COMPUTERS: THE "GERM EFFECT"

Based on the information provided above, one might assume that the mere existence of PCs, televisions, cell phones, and the like is the reason why there has been an explosion of information; they would be incorrect. The primary reason why there has been an "information explosion" over the last 10 years is because of the networking of PCs, including the Internet. In 1998, 82% of office PCs were networked. This number increased to 98% in 2006 (MBI). The increase of networked PCs facilitates the creation, discovery, use, and sharing of information at an exponential rate. These networked PCs lead to what I call the *Germ Effect* of information.

The *Germ Effect* of information occurs when a collective of information (that was originally created and shared by others prior in the chain) is used by *Person A*, who — because of the simplicity of information-sharing provided by networking — shares this information with several other users who repeat the process. Ultimately, this original collective of information has been shared and used by many. With a push of a button, electronic mail allows a single user to quickly and easily transmit information to potentially thousands of other users. Access to the Internet affords the user an easy means of researching, accessing, using, and ultimately sharing a virtual history database of information with a click of the mouse. The easy access to and transmittal of information via networked PCs is the primary reason for the exponential growth in information.

The reason why the growth of information is oftentimes referred to as the *Information Explosion* is because of the rate at which the volume of information has multiplied over such a short period of time. The amount of information generated between the years 1995 and 2000 is equal to the total volume of information that has been generated throughout all of history. The volume of information is expected to double every five years, so that between the years 2000 and 2005, the volume of information generated is expected to be twice the volume of information generated throughout history!

PAPER USAGE GROWTH IN THE UNITED STATES

SO WHAT? Why should you or I care about all of the information that is being generated? The answer: *paper output generation.* A Delphi Group study shows that 90% of information ultimately resides on paper in three distinct genres: books; serials (including newspapers, mass market and trade periodicals, scholarly periodicals and newsletters) and documents printed or copied in offices — the U.S. print information flow is dominated by office documents. Some studies estimate that as much as 95% of information resides on paper in corporations. Heck, the introduction of e-mail into organizations alone results — on average — in a 40% increase in paper consumption.

There is a direct correlation between the amount of information that is generated and the amount of paper consumed in the business office. Although the percentage of paper consumed in the U.S. decreases each year, the raw amount of paper continues to increase (albeit at a decreasing rate annually). Paper consumption used to outpace the growth of the US economy, but the past two or three years have seen a slowdown in sales. The growth rate of paper sales in the United States is flattening by about half a percent each year. Between 2004 and 2005 plain white office paper was expected to grow less than 4 percent (InfoTrends/CAP Ventures). However, some firms, such as Forest Ethics, estimate that the number of pages consumed by U.S. corporations is growing by about 20% each year. So I guess it's safe to say that paper consumption in the office is growing between 4% and 20% per year, depending on how you correlate paper sales and paper consumption in the office. But keep in mind that "paper sales" is not limited to the paper that is consumed in the office workplace. It can also include paper sold to newspaper and magazine printers and other such paper consumers.

The decline in the percentage of paper consumed in the office can be attributed to advances in digital infrastructures, databases/archiving and communication systems, and a new generation of tech-savvy workers who are more comfortable with the use and security of technology. However, one of the often most overlooked reasons why there has been a decline in the percentage of paper consumed in the office is because of the decline in the size of the U.S. labor force over the past 40 years.

Annual Growth Rate of the U.S. Labor Force

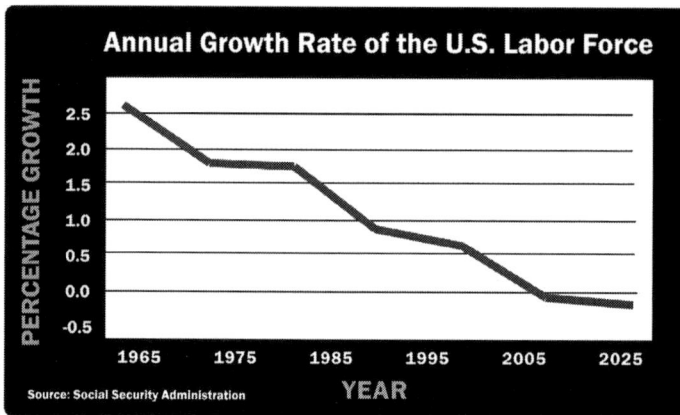

Source: Social Security Administration

To me, this raises an obvious question: what percentage of the decline in the growth rate of paper consumption is due to technology versus the reduction in the size of the labor force? Interesting, ain't it? Unfortunately, I will not posit an answer here, because the important thing to consider is that if the number of people in the workplace remained flat (as opposed to decreasing), it's almost a certainty that paper consumption in the office would be increasing at an increasing rate.

ADVANCEMENTS IN TECHNOLOGY

As strange as it may seem, the very things that are supposed to lessen our dependence on paper has, so far, been some of the main contributors to the increase in paper consumption.

Electronic communication technologies that are expected to help companies reduce the amount of paper output that is generated, actually facilitate paper production and encourage additional paper consumption. This is because these technologies which allow users to create, distribute and store *information* electronically, also provide users with more sources from which to propagate information and generate paper output.

Not too long ago, users had to hand-write or type (via *typewriter*, remember those?) if they wanted to convey information on paper. As a result, paper output generation and duplication were slow, somewhat difficult, and infrequent. With advancements in electronic technologies we now have printers, MFPs/copiers, fax machines, scanners, and other tools that offer the option of easily and quickly creating a paper copy of the information we use.

Some technologies will, in fact, live up to their advanced billing and lead to the reduction of both the percentage of paper consumed *and* the raw quantity. Back office applications that take advantage of Content Management solutions (including the document conversion process) can lead to the reduction of paper consumption *and* physical paper storage. The front office is where the growth in paper consumption continues to thrive in the face of technological advances.

ELECTRONIC MAIL: E-mail increases and facilitates the volume of communication and information exchange. E-mail messages are sent across networks to multiple users that reply to the messages received, make annotations, and send a reply to the sender; they also send carbon copies to other users. If this e-mail traffic is kept in electronic form, then the potential for paper reduction is greatest. However, most users at some point will print an email message. 94% of users I surveyed stated that they print e-mail messages for various reasons, the most frequently-stated reason is for storage of the hardcopy document as a record.

Twenty-five years ago, a document was printed once and manually routed to many people via some form of land mail or via fax machine. Today, documents are routed electronically to many people simultaneously *and* printed many times by many of the recipients. The result is that e-mail — a technology that is supposed to help reduce paper consumption — not only increases the amount of *information* that flows back-and-forth, but also increases the amount of paper output that is produced.

SCANNERS AND OTHER DIGITIZERS: Documents that are digitized using scanners and other digitizers are frequently used in conjunction with e-mail as attachments for transmission. In these instances, the scanned documents become more e-mail, and the same distribute—print process applies as described in the previous paragraph. In other words, a significant percentage of the documents that were originally digitized (taken out of paper form and converted to electronic form) will re-emerge as printed output.

FAX MACHINES: Even with the use of fax modems, e-Fax, and LAN-based fax (technologies that eliminate the paper-based fax job), the recipient of the fax transmission will oftentimes make a paper copy of the faxed document, even if it is received on their PC! Research shows that the types of documents that are frequently transmitted via fax machine in the workplace (e.g. invoices) are of such a nature that recipients feel the need to make a hardcopy back up for reference.

CORPORATE CONSUMPTION

Different studies reveal different levels of paper consumption by users in U.S. corporations. My research reveals that there is a spectrum on which sits two categories of paper consumers: *Conservative Paper Consumers* and *Prosperous Paper Consumers*.

I define "Conservative" Consumers as those companies that are performing moderately well financially and have stringent controls on office technology acquisition. "Prosperous" Consumers are those companies that are making lots of money and their controls on office technology acquisition are less stringent. For example, Prosperous Consumers typically allow departments with individual profit & loss responsibilities to purchase office technology — at their discretion — if the cost of the intended purchase is less than, say, $1,000. There also seems to be a correlation between the size of an organization and the associated paper consumption (and cost); large corporations tend to fall at the *prosperous* end of the spectrum, while smaller companies trend towards the *conservative* end of the scale. High paper-intensive companies (e.g. financial services companies, insurance companies and consulting firms) are also included at the *prosperous* end of the spectrum.

In *conservative* companies, each worker consumes an average of approximately 5,400 sheets of paper per year (BIS Strategic Decisions). Additional research (including studies I have performed at U.S. corporations) reveals that each user in *prosperous* companies consumes an average of approximately 14,100 pages annually at the high end. Assessment engagements I have performed show the average number of pages consumed per-user annually is about 8,695 paged per year.

How are we generating paper output in the office? Typically, information is transferred to paper output using printers, copiers/multi-function devices (a.k.a. Multi-function Peripherals or MFPs), and fax machines. In 1996, the amount of printed pages exceeded the amount of (on-glass) copied pages for the first time in history. In 2002, printed pages accounted for 70% of the total number of pages produced on printers and copiers combined; copied pages represented the remaining 30% of pages. Today, based on distributed office output assessments I have performed, the percentage of printed-to-copied pages is in the neighborhood of 76%-to-24%. When looking at the total number of pages printed (including pages printed on multi-function devices), copied (on-glass), and faxed (received) in the distributed office environment, the ratios are approximately as follows: print = 74%; copy = 24%; and fax= 2% of pages (Oxford Hill Consulting, 2006).

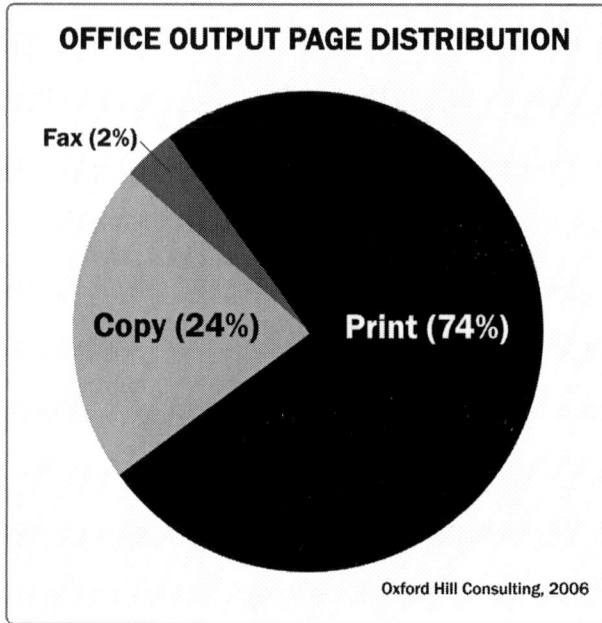

OFFICE OUTPUT PAGE DISTRIBUTION

Fax (2%)

Copy (24%)

Print (74%)

Oxford Hill Consulting, 2006

chapter two
FROM MY COLD DEAD HANDS!

REMEMBER THE "PAPERLESS OFFICE"? How's that workin' out? With all of the advancements in digital technology you would think that our reliance on (or should I say our *desire for*) that physical piece of paper would wane, but, although our use of paper is increasing at a decreasing rate, it's still increasing. Why is that? Why can't we get away from that piece of paper? The simple answer: we *like* paper (also referred to as "hardcopy")!

According to the Bureau of Labor Statistics, the average age of the workforce has *increased* from 35-years old in 1979 to 41-years old in 2005. That's right, the workforce is *aging* as opposed to getting younger.

An Aging Workforce—Change in Numbers of U.S. Workers			
Age of Worker	1970 – 1980	1990 – 2000	1996 – 2006
20 – 24	50%	-5%	14%
25 – 34	72	-14	-9
35 – 44	24	18	-3
45 – 54	0	51	25
55 – 64	5	22	54
Over 65	-6	14	9
Source: U.S. Census Bureau and Bureau of Labor Statistics			

However, over the next 5-to-10 years or so, that number should be coming down and younger, more tech-savvy workers will dominate. But until that time, older folks rule. And these older folks grew up with paper. When we were kids, we learned to read from paper (books, magazines, etc.), we learned to write on paper, we did our homework on paper, we edited book reports directly on the paper, we applied to college on paper applications, we paid our bills on paper, read our news on paper, we know how to file & store paper ... got the idea? Over the first two-thirds of our lives we have interacted with paper and have grown comfortable with it; we *know* paper intimately and we have developed a habit of living with it.

It wasn't until we were in college that the use of technology became familiar to us, and a digital infrastructure (converting paper-based processes to electronic) is still not totally trusted by this older generation of workers.

Even today, in this age of technology, the use of paper still makes things easier, is more convenient, and is more trusted by some people than electronic options. How much fun is it to read a 20-page document on you computer? Not much. How convenient is it to review and edit a 30-page report on your computer screen? Not very. How convenient is it to whip out your PC and read the daily news, or your PC? Not as convenient as it is to do so on paper, I imagine.

Paper is flexible; we can fold it up, put it in our pocket, slide it in our brief cases and pocket books, and read it during our morning commute — even when you're standing on the crowded E-train headed Uptown in New York city. We can take notes on paper, highlight things on paper, write in the margins on paper, use markers, pens, and crayons on paper, and then give it to someone else who can in turn easily read the document and your notes.

And when it comes time to store our paper for safe-keeping, we know how to do that, too. And when we file away our paper documents, we have confidence that it will remain safely-stored in that location until we need to retrieve it — even if our PC hard drive crashes and burns.

The bottom line is that no matter how technologically-advanced our office infrastructures become, the older workers will still have an affinity for that physical piece of paper. And because we have such an affinity, we will continue to create paper output of information at a rate that is somewhat commensurate with the growth in information. And the only way (at least in the short-term) that you're going to get us totally away from this reliance on paper is by removing it *from our cold, dead hands!* In other words, as long as we're in the workforce, we're gonna demand paper output, so keep the printers comin'!

chapter three
PAPER OUTPUT CREATION DEVICE GROWTH

PRINTER GROWTH

The U.S. single-function printer market grew 6% in 2005 (based on units shipped), from 2004. This includes the color and monochrome laser segment and inkjet printers across all segments. Color printers experienced the fastest growth in the general office with an estimated 56% year-over-year growth rate between 2003 and 2004 (InfoTrends). As the cost for single-function color laser printers continues to decline (less than $1,000) and as companies begin to realize the benefits of color output and the ease with which they can now do many color jobs in-house, color printers are being purchased at an increasing rate year-over-year, while single-function monochrome printers' sales get cannibalized. Single-function color laser printers are now the fastest growing segment of the printer market. It's inevitable that, over time (ten years?), single-function monochrome laser printers will be priced comparable to color laser printers (or some new form of color ink technology) on a cost-per-page basis, and companies will simply stop purchasing the monochrome printers.

MFP/COPIER GROWTH

Workgroup color laser MFPs grew approximately 47% between 2003 and 2004, and color laser MFPs across all segments continue to be the fastest growing segment of MFPs. The central reprographics/production class MFP grew more than 70% between 2003 and 2004, and it is estimated that color MFPs in the production segment increased by more than 200% during this same period! As prices and the technology improve, more and more companies are bringing outsourced print jobs in-house as a means of saving money. When they do this, they also bring along production-class color MFPs.

Let me step back for a minute: when I refer to a multifunction peripheral/device (MFP), I am including what we commonly refer to as "copiers" in this category. To me, the distinction between a "copier" and a "MFP" is that *copiers* allow the user to place a piece of paper on a glass surface of a copy machine and make duplicates; that's it. You cannot print to these devices from your desktop and you can't do any scanning or faxing from a "copier." A *copier* is a single-function device that is not network-attachable. In fact, I don't believe that any manufacturer even makes single-function, non-networkable (analog) office copiers anymore.

When I refer to a device as a "MFP," I am talking about a device that you can attach to the network, and users can send print jobs to it just like a printer; they can walk-up and make on-glass copies, just like a "copier"; and they can also use the device for scanning and sending faxes.

The cost of MFPs and even digital offset color printers have become reasonable, and companies see this as an opportunity to reduce operational costs by bringing the appropriate print jobs in-house. In addition, with the growth of digital processes and Internet/web-based print service providers, companies are discovering alternatives for satisfying their printing needs. The effect of companies bringing outsourced print jobs such as marketing collateral in-house is being felt by commercial printers. According to The National Association of Printing Leadership, the estimated number of commercial printers still in business (printing companies that perform outsourced print services for corporations) has decreased by 25% between 1998 and 2007.

Number of Commercial Printing Establishments (1998-2007)							
	Estimated		Actual			Percent Loss	
Employees	2007	2003	2001	2000	1998	'01/'98	'00/'98
Total	28,199	32,022	34,172	35,016	37,673	9.3%	7.1%
Less than 10	18,549	21,052	22,482	22,884	24,816	-9.4%	-7.8%
10 to 19	3,903	4,576	4,938	5,102	5,535	-10.8%	-7.8%
20 to 49	3,124	3,553	3,789	3,980	4,174	-9.2%	-4.6%
50 to 99	1,307	1,476	1,568	1,644	1,718	-8.7%	-4.3%
100 or more	1,332	1,342	1,352	1,363	1,373	-1.5%	-0.8%
Source: National Association of Printing Leadership (NAPL)							

FAX AND SCANNER GROWTH

In 2005, scan-enabled solutions (high-speed digital imaging, network-attached scanners and MFPs) grew 31%. As more digital applications (such as document management solutions) become adopted by companies, there will be an increased need to get paper-based documents into digital format by using scanning functionality.

The market for fax machines continues to shrink and shipment growth (as a percentage) trends downward year-over-year. Small format and personal fax machines' growth has been consumed by workgroup mid-sized formats (growing at a little over 1% annually) primarily due to price reductions; you can now get a workgroup class fax machine for under $50 on eBay. In addition, workgroup MFPs with analog fax capability are rendering single-function fax machines obsolete, while fax service providers are showing companies how they can reduce their cost of faxing by eliminating their fax machines altogether.

chapter four
BUT WHERE DOES IT ALL GO?

COMPANIES GENERATE TONS OF INFORMATION, create boat-loads of paper output, and spend millions of dollars on printers and print services. Where does it all go? How much of the volume of paper created annually is created in the general office? The central reprographics department? The data center? How much is sent outside to print service providers? Where is the percentage of spend for these categories of output going? To answer these questions, we first need to define each of these segments based on the context in which I will use them throughout this document.

DISTRIBUTED OFFICE

The distributed (general) office is the part of the organization where the end-users create, print, copy, fax, scan, and finish (e.g. collate, staple) the pages and documents they use in the course of doing their jobs. End-users typically send output jobs from their PCs to the self-service printers and workgroup MFPs located throughout the general office environment.

PRODUCTION/CENTRAL REPROGRAPHICS

The production environment (also referred to as the *Central Reproduction Department* — CRD, the print shop, and the copy center) is the in-house part of the company where high-volume document production and duplication is performed. Sometimes, the mailroom function is a part of this environment.

Companies encourage users to direct print and reproduction jobs of certain sizes to the appropriate environment. For instance, some companies will instruct users to create output jobs of 100-pages or less in the general office, while sending larger, more complex jobs to the production environment. Normally, the high-speed, high-volume MFPs used in this environment require an operator to run them.

DATA CENTER AND MAINFRAME

The output that is produced in the data center off of mainframe (large) computer systems is normally created on "green-bar" (impact) printers and high-speed cut-sheet printers. End-users rarely have access to these printers for use in creating their day-to-day output. Mainframe printers produce large reports and system data that are used by data center managers and other IT professionals. Many times, companies will tie several printers together (clustering) to achieve extremely high speeds of printer output creation.

COMMERCIAL/EXTERNAL PRINT

Commercial printing (also referred to as external printing and print service provider printing) includes marketing collateral, brochures, booklets, annual reports, forms, labels, and other "professional" print requirements. This is the category of printing that is outsourced and performed by printing companies (print service providers) that are not owned by the corporation requesting the print jobs.

An emerging sub-category of the external print spend category is Internet-based print service providers that allow end-users to electronically submit print jobs over the Internet to be fulfilled by 3rd party printers.

THE BLACK HOLE

The reality is that in most large corporations, there will inevitably be a percentage of printed output for which the company cannot account. No one seems to know where the pages went or came from, or how much money was spent on the "lost" pages. But they all will agree that they produce and pay for some percentage of pages that they absolutely cannot account for.

Based on actual study data gathered from output assessments that I have performed over the years, in addition to 2006 research data provided by Oxford Hill Consulting (across multiple industries), a general break-out of pages and costs (there is an assumption of a direct correlation between the number of pages produced in an environment and their associated costs) can be described as presented in the table below. Please keep in mind that the percentage break-outs provided below are a summary across multiple industries, and could differ somewhat from the percentages in your specific industry.

Corporate Paper Production and Spend by Segment	
Distributed/General Office = 20.2%	20.2%
Production/CRD = 5.1%	5.1%
Data center/Mainframe = 2.4%	2.4%
Commercial/External Print = 70.6%	70.6%
Other and/or unaccounted for = 1.7%	1.7%
[1]Tab Edwards studies. [2]Oxford Hill Consulting, 2006	

PART TWO

....

THE DISTRIBUTED OFFICE

The focus of this book will be on the **DISTRIBUTED OFFICE ENVIRONMENT.** The "distributed office" can simply be described as the general office work environment where employees have local, easy access to the use of printers, convenience (self-service), MFPs and copiers, and fax machines.

chapter five
SO WHAT?

YOU MAY BE ASKING YOURSELF: "SO WHAT? So the end-users are generating lots of information leading to lots of paper output-demand leading to lots of printer and MFP purchases?" The part you can't leave off is: "… leading to **LOTS OF DOLLARS SPENT SUPPORTING THIS OUTPUT DEMAND!"**

For many years the distributed office output environment (consisting mainly of printers, self-serve copiers, fax machines and scanners) remained one of the last areas of the Information technology (IT) organization to be studied, measured, and analyzed for inefficiency and cost-savings. Even to this day, many companies have not investigated this part of the organization for potential efficiency improvements. The reasons many IT managers give for this seeming lack of interest are: because printers are inexpensive; they don't break very often, and when they do, it's easier to just get a new one than it is to worry about it; printing, office copying and faxing are "small potatoes" in relation to the other, more pressing IT issues they have to deal with; they don't know how to begin to measure and analyze the office output environment; and my all-time favorite: so what the printer is broken? Users shouldn't be printing that much paper *anyway*!

What these IT managers don't fully understand is that there is significant waste and inefficiency in the office output environment, and that the space is rife with opportunities to eliminate waste, reduce costs and improve end-user productivity.

HOW BAD IS IT, DOC?

In all of my years of experience in helping companies analyze their output environments and become more efficient in their use of paper output, one universal truth is that most companies don't know how bad the "problem" really is. The "problem" to which I refer is multifaceted and includes high costs, unhappy users, waste, inefficiency, and poor management and administration.

TOTAL COST OF OWNERSHIP (TCO) is the true cost (both "hard" and "soft") of acquiring and owning an asset, and making that asset available to users over an extended period of time. "Hard" costs are costs for which a company outlays real currency — "foldin' money" as I refer to it. It is a cost whose payment can be traced to an actual cash outflow on a financial statement. In other words, you have to physically send someone money to pay a *hard* cost. Examples of *hard costs* include: purchase & lease costs, phone line charges, power consumption costs, and the costs of consumables. "Soft" costs are typically those dollar *values* associated with the amount of time someone spends on an activity — converted into a dollar amount. For example, each day, John Doe wastes 3 hours trying to fix the copy machine. Translated into *soft* costs (using an hourly pay rate of $50), we can say that each day, the company loses $150 due to the fact that John Doe has to fix the copy machine in order to get his copy jobs completed. The $150 in this example is a *soft* cost, because it doesn't involve any actual physical cash outlay (a.k.a. *hard* dollars).

COST-PER-PAGE. When companies want to break TCO down into a unit of measure that they can use for relative comparison purposes, they will divide the TCO of an output device by the number of pages produced on the device over a measured period, and calculate the Cost-Per-Page (CPP). So, if a printer costs $1,000 per month to own & operate (the TCO), and that printer produces 2,000 pages per month, then the monthly cost-per-page for that printer is fifty-cents ($0.50) per-page. **THIS IS IMPORTANT: Using this example, it should become clear how the CPP can (and almost always will) be different for every same-model device, because it's based on the TCO of that device. And the TCO of a device is based on many factors, such as the pages produced on the device and the various costs applied to a device. This means that applying a blanket statement such as: "The cost-per-page of the competitive Brand X printer is higher than the cost-per-page of my company's Brand Y printer" is misleading.**

By the definition of TCO as provided in the above paragraph, it should be evident that the true total cost of having a shared printer or MFP in the office is more than the obvious costs of the purchase price of the asset, the cost of maintenance, and the cost of the consumables (e.g. ink and toner) and supplies (e.g. maintenance kits and drum units). When I consult with companies, I always try to get them to understand this concept right up front — and it ain't always easy.

One way that I have found effective in helping companies understand and buy-into the concept of "total cost" is by asking them to brainstorm a laundry list of answer the following question:

Assume that your company got rid of every printer, copier, and fax machine in the company. In other words, you now have zero printers, zero copiers and zero fax machines throughout your company. If this were the case, which costs that you presently incur (because you own printers, copiers, and fax machines) will you no longer have to incur?

After I ask this question, the participants typically inundate me with different costs that the company would avoid if they had no printers, copiers or fax machines installed. These cost elements include:

- The purchase price or lease costs of the devices
- The cost of paper
- The cost of supplies and consumables
- Maintenance costs
- Power consumption costs
- Phone line, port and per-call charges
- Network port costs
- Printer-related network management costs
- Installation costs
- Print servers and software license costs
- Helpdesk costs
- Asset management costs
- Floor space/real-estate costs
- Personnel costs/key operator costs
- User training costs
- Various productivity and soft costs, etc.

The TCO cost elements and cost factors that I recommend using for calculating the Total Cost of Ownership for distributed office output are provided in the table below:

TCO Elements	Descriptive Information
Hardware	Acquisition costs (lease, rent or purchase), annual depreciation (device age is important here), expensed cost threshold. Remember to include print servers.
Software	License costs, upgrades, customization
Supplies and consumables	Paper, toner (percent color and mono), drum units, ink cartridges, maintenance kits
IT management	Installation, integration, re-boxing, deinstallation and disposal, network costs and IP connectivity (per network-attached device), management of hard-copy devices, asset management, driver installation and configuration, server management
Facilities costs	Power consumption (considering power save modes), physical space (costs for space for floor-standing equipment), upgrade costs (e.g. adding power outlets, platforms, etc), phone line and port charges, purchasing costs
Document production	The user workflow action (create, print, retrieve, copy, fax, return), user training, document delivery
Maintenance and support	Preventative maintenance, break-fix service, warranty and warranty-extensions, on-site support personnel
Helpdesk costs	Level-0, level-1 and level-2 helpdesk support

When you consider all of the aforementioned costs that companies incur by simply owning printers, copiers and fax machines and making them available to users over time — the Total Cost of Ownership — you begin to comprehend the magnitude of the potential cost problem in the environment.

DOCUMENT PRODUCTION COST: An efficiency measure that is starting to make the rounds in consulting circles is the concept of *Document Production Cost* (DPC). Document Production Costing is a model that incorporates both the *hard* dollar and *soft* dollar cost variables into the calculation of what it really "costs" to *produce* a document. So, using the aforementioned example of John Doe, if the hard dollar cost of the documents that John creates in a day is $25, and the soft dollar cost associated with John having to fix the copier in order to get his output job completed is $150, then the total Document Production Cost for the documents that John creates on that day is $175.

Proponents of the use of the DPC calculation argue that if you take into consideration the amount of time it takes an end-user to create and produce a document — in addition to the other costs associated with that document — then and only then will you have captured what it truly costs a company to have its users operate within the hardcopy infrastructure that is in place.

I believe that the value of using DPC lies in the fact that it forces companies to consider not only the physical device infrastructure and their associated costs, but it also forces companies to look at ways to improve the user workflow experience and offer an environment that improves user productivity.

WASTE AND INEFFICIENCY: Although the costs are the most attention-grabbing aspect of output device ownership, the waste and excess capacity can also be a revelation. For instance, based on my study data, the overall average user-to-device ratio in a typical company is 3.5-to-1 (for print, copy and fax combined). That means that each device in the company supports about 3 people. And for printers, the average ratio is 4-to-1. These are relatively low, inefficient ratios. Some consulting firms recommend a user-to-printer ratio of at least 10-to-1, and I've even seen some as high as 15-to-1.

Okay, okay, I know: in and of themselves, user-to-devices don't really mean much, and you shouldn't design a device deployment based solely on what some wacky consultant says is a good ratio. True, the value of a device-to-ratio can only be appreciated when you consider that ratio in the context of other available information. I have performed numerous assessments where the existing user-to-device ratios were below 5-to-1, but in these environments that ratio suited the demand for hardcopy output in those companies. That's why it is of utmost importance to consider each measure of efficiency (e.g. device-to-user ratios, average pages-per-device-per-month, user requirements, and cost-per-page - TCO divided by the number of pages produced), to form a complete picture of the level of inefficiency in the environment.

These measures of (in)efficiency can tell you many things about the level of waste and excess capacity (leading to relatively high costs) in the print, MFP/copy and fax infrastructure within your company, including:

- The age and level of age-related inefficiency of a device
- The level of waste (excess capacity and/or under-utilization) in usage of the devices
- The high cost (TCO) of a device
- The degree of fit between the device fleet and user requirements
- The level of workflow and user-related work process inefficiency
- The general inefficiency in the fleet design/layout and device deployment
- The effect of lack of sufficient fleet management and administration

Let's humor the "ratio consultants" for a minute (yeah, I'm a consultant, too, so you can lump me into this category if you want to). Suppose a theoretical efficient ratio of users-to-devices in a particular company is 10-to-1. Now suppose that an assessment of the office output environment in that company revealed an *actual* ratio of 4-to-1. Assuming that other findings from the assessment support the notion of a 4-to-1 ratio being inefficient, then this company would have 2.5 times more devices than they need if based on the theoretical 10-to-1 ratio.

So, if the company has 20,000 users and 5,000 devices, then based on this scenario, the company would have 3,000 devices too many! And when you consider the time, effort and cost associated with maintaining these 3,000 extra (unnecessary) devices, you can see how having excess capacity can be a burden to a company.

USER PRODUCTIVITY: One of the major problems that results from the failure to periodically assess and proactively manage the office output environment is that user requirements for effective document-related solutions often go unmet. In a typical inefficient distributed office, users can spend hours per month wasting time unnecessarily "walking paper." It's called wasted time "walking paper" because many of the steps a user has to go through to produce and retrieve his or her output may be unnecessary (wasted time) if an efficient document-related infrastructure was in place.

For example, a user sends a print job from his or her PC to the network-attached single-function printer. The user walks to the printer to retrieve the print-job, and then walks the job over to the copy room to make some copies of the document and have them stapled. After that, the user may need to send a copy of the documents to a co-worker, so the user walks the pages from the copy room to the fax machine and sends the fax pages. And if the user is like me, the user will stand and watch the fax machine (this can take up to 6-minutes) to make sure that the pages were sent successfully. After sending the fax, the user then walks back to his or her desk. That entire round-trip can take upwards of 12-minutes (depending on the device locations on the floor), and most of those activities are avoidable given today's available technology and knowledge.

So if this user produces an average of 3 output jobs per day, and follows this same process each time, then the user wastes 12-hours per month walking paper. And using an hourly-pay rate of $50, it costs the company

$600 per month (in *soft* or DPC productivity costs) for this one employee — not to mention the level of user frustration and dissatisfaction associated with the time wasted creating and distributing documents.

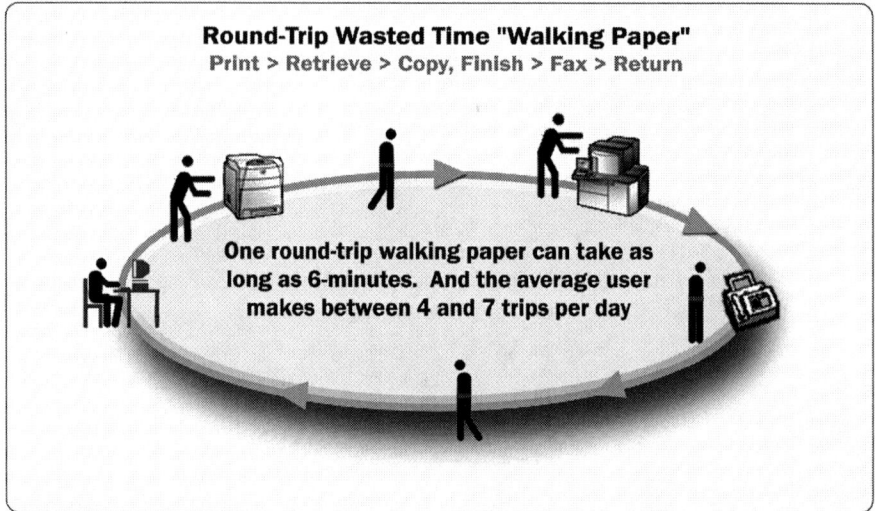

Round-Trip Wasted Time "Walking Paper"
Print > Retrieve > Copy, Finish > Fax > Return

One round-trip walking paper can take as long as 6-minutes. And the average user makes between 4 and 7 trips per day

chapter six
PAPER PROBLEMS

IN THE PREVIOUS CHAPTER, WE DISCUSSED some of the reasons why companies should care about the goings-on in the distributed office output environment, including: high costs, waste & inefficiency, and the negative effect on user productivity.

But there's another set of issues derived from the fact that end-users need to create so much output in the course of doing their jobs. These are the challenges facing companies by virtue of the fact that they must create and use so much physical paper in the course of conducting business. These challenges — in conjunction with the problems of cost and inefficiency described in the previous chapter — I refer to as *Paper Problems*.

THE PAPER TRAIL. When information is discovered, created and/or shared, most of it eventually gets transcribed onto a physical piece of paper. When people produce paper output, they *do* something with it. But what do they do with it? According to MBI, the disposition of paper output that has been created in the general office flows like this:

THE PAPER TRAIL What ultimately happens to paper produced in the office?	
Filed/stored as paper	32.8%
Discarded	30.2%
Transferred to someone else	14.6%
Lost (70% must be re-produced)	10.0%
Converted to digital form and stored	11.3%
Other	1.10%
SOURCE: Marketing & Business Integration (MBI), LLC. Study: *Follow That Paper!*, 2005	

FILED/STORED

PAPER STORAGE. Because we create paper, we inevitably have to (or want to) file a third of these documents away for safe-keeping. Most end-users store paper on their desks, on shelves, in filing cabinets, in records rooms, and even in long-term storage facilities — including locations in a different building. We store paper for lots of reasons ranging from our desire to store a keep-sake, to the need to make paper available on-demand for legal reasons. And paper storage does have a cost associated with it. These costs can include the cost of the file cabinets, the cost of the storage containers, the cost-per-square-foot of real estate, the cost of labor to manage the filing operation, and the cost of renting a storage facility.

The cost of renting or leasing a separate facility just to store paper documents is not unheard of. I recall a story of how several years ago a Fortune 5 company saved millions of dollars by implementing an optical storage solution. The interesting thing about the cost savings was that they came *from not having to lease the hangar-sized warehouse where the paper documents had been stored!*

Costs are one part of the equation, but of the most annoying aspects of storing documents is the amount of time users waste traveling to the storage location, searching for documents, filing documents, and re-creating those documents they misplaced; it's a pain in the ass!

Electronic Storage. While the cost of disk storage media steadily decreases, it is often outweighed by total disk storage growth in many customer IT environments. The reality is that as long as we continue to increase our paper production — and as more paper documents get converted to digital documents — we will probably continue to increase our spend for storage media. However, a compelling aspect of electronic storage is the ability to easily store, search for, and retrieve documents; this is helping to sooth that *pain.*

Regulatory Compliance. Although there are no real regulatory requirements for the type of storage media companies can use (unless you're a securities broker or trader doing business in the United States), there are nonetheless a multitude of regulatory requirements that affect the way companies handle and manage documents. Different industries must comply with different regulations that affect the way companies manage e-mail, archive documents, backup, recover, and secure documents.

DISCARDED. Approximately one-third of all pages produced in the general office are discarded. Why? There are many reasons for it, but the few that immediately come to mind when I think of wasted pages are: pages that were printed but never needed (such as duplicate print jobs); pages that were received, printed or copied and were only needed for a single point in time (such "proofs" and handouts); and pages — that were given to us by another user — for which we have no use (such as sales collateral and "FYI" copies of documents).

TRANSFERRED TO SOMEONE ELSE. This is especially an issue in the Legal and Financial communities where there are several "need-to-know" recipients or people whose signatures and approvals are required.

LOST. Some studies I have seen actually conclude that about one out of every ten pages that are printed/copied are eventually lost. The implication: They must be re-created leading to duplicate costs (or worse, if the documents were valuable).

These are just some of the conditions (or should I say *consequences*) of producing paper in the course of conducting business. And because we must (that's right, we *must*) produce paper in the course of conducting business), we are inevitably faced with the following conditions:

- Waste & high costs
- Inefficiency
- Operational ineffectiveness
- Poor Quality of Service
- Regulatory requirements

Then, we are faced with the challenge of having to *do* something about. And when we investigate possible solutions to improve the paper problems, we soon realize that it's probably gonna cost us lots of money, lots of time, and lots of headaches.

"HOW DID IT GET TO THIS POINT? Where did we go wrong? I was so busy with work that I didn't pay as much attention as I should have." No, it's not the voice of someone reflecting on a relationship gone bad. It's actually the kinds of questions IT managers find themselves asking when they realize their office output environments are in shambles.

What's interesting is that most IT managers instinctively realize they might have a hardcopy efficiency problem in the distributed office, even though they may not have formally performed any type of analysis or assessment of the environment. Oftentimes, it's just a matter of walking the floors, looking at the rows of printers and fax machines lined-up next to each other on a table, seeing all of the stacks of leftover printed and copied pages lurking around the devices and in trash cans, and ducking the flying objects being thrown at you by the disgruntled end-users as they see you walking by.

So how might a company's hardcopy environment have ended up in a condition as described above? The possible reasons are many, but my experience in working with companies to understand this problem has shown that there are a handful of reasons that consistently show up as contributing to an inefficient hardcopy environment.

- **DEPARTMENTAL PURCHASE AUTONOMY.** When individual departments have local budgets and the autonomy to purchase anything they want as long as the cost of the item is within the pre-approved expense limit (typically $1,000 or less), then users will inevitably go to the local technology store and buy a printer if their print output requirements aren't being met by the IT or facilities department. If, for instance, a user needs color printing capability and there is no color functionality conveniently available to that user, then the user will simply go to the local Staples and purchase a $199 color inkjet printer. And, of course, once the user has the printer in his or her office, they will have it added to the corporate service and supplies contracts, creating additional expense for the company.

- **THE OL' "CONFIDENTIAL PRINTING" STORY.** Over the years, I have conducted numerous end-user office output surveys. One of the questions I ask is: "why do you have a personal printer?" (A "personal" printer is defined as a non-shared printer that is only being used by one person). In 90% of the cases, the user states that he or she "needs" the personal printer because they print lots of confidential documents. However, when I inform them that they can do confidential printing on the department's shared printers, the user will shift gears and give me another … uh … *reason* why they *need* that personal printer. What I have also learned is that by telling one's manager that they *need* a personal printer for confidential printing, the purchase approval rate is near 100%. The end result is that lots of people now have personal printers for … *confidential* printing requirements.

- **PRINTERS INFREQUENTLY BREAK.** When performing an output assessment, I always notice a high percentage of printers that are 5-years of age or older. In a typical environment, 42% of printers are of this age. The reason is because the installed printers, on the whole, rarely ever fail, so as long as they're still cranking out paper, why replace it? Most companies don't, but there are lots of reasons why it makes sense to replace old devices: they're more costly to operate; they use supplies and consumables less efficiently; the mean-time-between-failure starts to decrease, leading to higher service costs and user complaints; they often lack new, productivity-enhancing features; and they never go away!

- **DEVICES BECOME HAND-ME-DOWNS.** When users and/or departments get new printers, they rarely get rid of the old printer they are replacing. Instead, the old printer (which still works just fine) is offered up to other users or departments who may be able to use the printer. And, of course, when someone asks: "Hey, does anyone want a printer?" There is never a shortage of takers. The result is that old printers never go away, the ratio of users-to-devices decreases, the company's overall TCO increases because you are adding more printers, and eventually, user complaints will increase as the old printers get even older and start to break more frequently.

- **LACK OF INFRASTRUCTURE MANAGEMENT.** I estimate that 75% of companies don't actively manage and administer their office output device fleets, they don't use asset management tools, and they can't tell you — with any degree of accuracy — the number of devices or device manufacturers' products they have installed. Without sufficient controls in place, it's easy for an output environment to get out of control.

- **MORE PRESSING PROBLEMS TO ADDRESS.** Let's face it: printers, copiers and fax machines — nuisance hardcopy devices — have not traditionally been very high on the CIO's project list — mainly due to the perception that it was a low-dollar value part of the IT infrastructure. Recently, though, companies are paying more attention to this space since numerous studies have come out showing how companies can save millions of dollars by effectively streamlining and managing the office output environment of the company. But for many years, the hardcopy environment has been neglected, and like any neglected resource, years of neglect can lead to enormous problems.

- **ANALOG COPIERS ARE CHEAP.** Companies looking to save money will find the thought of adding old, outdated analog copiers to their fleet somewhat appealing. I am not aware of any company today that makes new analog (non-digital, non-network-attachable, single-function) workgroup-class (and above) copiers. However, in about 65% of the assessments I perform at companies, I always discover them. The main reason why companies use analog copiers is because they're very inexpensive. Suppliers that provide analog copiers typically keep a stockpile of these off-lease, refurbished devices in inventory. The devices have already been depreciated so they are not really a financial burden on the supplier. The toner cartridges used for these copiers are usually remanufactured, so they, too, are inexpensive. The result is that suppliers can offer analog copiers to companies for tenths of a cent per-page, including maintenance. So a desperate company looking to reduce the cost of output might find the addition of analog copiers attractive. Users be damned!

- **FAX MACHINES ARE CHEAP, FRIENDLY AND THEY WORK.** Analog fax machines (those that use analog phone lines for transmission) are not all bad: They're basically free; all users know how to use them and they are comfortable with their use; some trading partners still required that faxed pages be sent to them; and if the network goes down, you might not b able to use your e-mail account, but you can still send and receive fax pages. I have worked with companies whose users refused to even learn how to use more advanced forms of fax/document transmission because they are comfortable with using the fax machine. As a result, they never go away.

- **LACK OF ALIGNMENT BETWEEN IT AND FACILITIES.** For many years, the IT organization managed printers and the network, while the Facilities (Real Estate, Purchasing, Procurement) department managed copiers and fax machines. But when MFPs were introduced, you suddenly had a device that was both a printer and a copier/fax machine. So, since the MFP is like a network-attached printer, the IT organization felt justified in buying, installing, and managing them. And since the MFP is like a copier, the Facilities organization continued to buy them, too. (Let's ignore for the moment the in-fighting that took place between these two entities as the Facilities organization was buying devices that must then be installed and managed by the IT organization). Eventually you had situations where — unbeknownst to the other — both entities were buying MFPs. The result was that there were often twice as many devices being purchased than were needed. This situation is not as dicey today, as both entities have found a way to play nice.

I'm sure if I thought about it long enough I could come up with more reasons why so many companies' distributed office output environments are in such disarray (such as changes in end-user job-related workflow processes). But the list of reasons provided above contains the major contributors to the current levels of hardcopy inefficiency.

chapter eight
THINK, KNOW, PROVE

AS COMPANIES BEGIN THE QUEST TO UNDERSTAND the level of efficiently with which their distributed office output environment is operating, they should be reminded that — as they do so — it is of utmost importance that they be completely *honest* at all stages of the pursuit. Most people would say something like: "I *always* approach my job with honesty," or "That goes without saying." But in reality, it is very difficult for some managers to accept the possibility that the departments that they have been managing, overseeing, and/or supporting over the years have been deteriorating on their watch. An unfavorable diagnosis is like saying to the manager: "How did you let our company get like this? Your negligence has been costing us millions!" Well, maybe not that harsh, but I think you get the idea. If not, then maybe this true story will help paint the picture.

Some years ago, I was invited by a corporate executive to perform an office output assessment of the company's distributed environment. He was interested in seeing whether or not his company could cut the costs of output. Before conducting the assessment, I spoke with the company's IT manager who was responsible for the distributed office output environment at the company. The IT manager was a little irritated by the fact that he was being asked to support this analysis effort by his superiors at the company. He felt that if anyone should bring in external resources to perform such a study, it should be him. And besides, he believed that he was running a pretty efficient operation and that there was no need to waste time and money on this assessment. I understood his position and frustration, but I was hired by his boss's boss, so I had to do my job.

Anyway, after I had performed the assessment and analyzed the findings, I was ready to present my findings to the executives who were all gathered in a conference room; the IT manager was also in attendance. Before the presentation, I offered to review my preliminary findings with the IT manager, but he was not interested. So, I went ahead with the presentation and shared my unflattering findings with the executive team. It seemed that every time I presented an area of significant waste and inefficiency, the executives looked at the IT manager as if to say: "Didn't you know about that? If not, *why* didn't you know about that?" It was pretty painful to watch, but I imagine it was even more so for the IT manager. He looked as if he wanted to crawl under a rock and hide. He even disputed some of the findings from the study in an attempt to make himself look not-as-bad. And even after explaining my study methodology (which all of the executives had accepted and agreed was rational), the IT manager refused to accept the fact that the company's distributed office output environment was inefficient. This was an example of a manager not being honest with himself that he could have a problem of such a magnitude.

Over the years, I have come to rely on certain honesty-checking activities to help ensure that — as I performed certain consulting engagements — I was proceeding based on facts that I could prove (or at least rationally explain why one piece of data was more valid than another), and not based on information that *seemed* like it should be the right answer. The honesty-checking activities to which I refer introduce the *"Think? Know? Prove?"* (T-K-P) concept and are designed to force an added level of diligence and rigor to critical phases of projects. What we *Think* (what we believe or suppose), our level of *Knowledge* (familiarity, awareness, or understanding gained through experience or study) and that for which we have *Proof* (the act of validating; finding or testing the truth of something) can be used as measures of the level of diligence we apply to the stages of any project, whether it's an office assessment, a strategy development effort, or any basic problem-solving endeavor.

In my opinion, subjecting certain aspects of the problem-solving process to this rigor helps companies get an honest view of where they may need to do more work before they can have a clear and honest assessment of their prospect for solving a problem. Stages of a project that pass the T-K-P rigor are, in my opinion, more credible when presented to management. But it's not just in the business place where T-K-P yields answers (and ultimately results) that are more credible and trustworthy, but we can apply it to our daily lives.

Let's assume that your car is making a "strange" noise, so you take your car to three mechanics. You describe the noise to Mechanic #1 who says: "Based on your description, I *think* I know what your problem is. It's called the *Cat* noise." You then take your car to Mechanic #2 who asks you to start your car so that she can listen to the "strange" noise. She takes a listen and says: "Based on my experience, I *know* what your problem is. It's called the *Dog* noise." Next, you take your can to Mechanic #3 who hooks your car up to some machine and says: "I've run some tests, and I can *prove* what that noise is. It's called a *Bird* noise." Which mechanic's diagnosis would you have the most confidence in as being correct? Probably Mechanic #3.

In the fields of scientific enquiry, researchers often form hypotheses in the early stages of their quests for answers and solutions to problems. As information becomes available, researchers will often apply the T-K-P check against the data and other suggestions to help decide whether or not the data qualify for consideration.

For example, let's assume that some research scientist was fed up with listening to vegetarians rant about how they only eat vegetables because they "could never harm another living creature." So, in order to silence those vegetarians, the scientist developed a hypothesis that he has always believed: *plants are living "creatures" that feel pain, too.* Applying the T-K-P rule against this hypothesis, you get the following:

HYPOTHESIS: PLANTS ARE LIVING CREATURES THAT FEEL PAIN

1. What do you THINK? I think that plants feel pain

2. What do you KNOW? We know that plants, including vegetables, feel pain when subjected to trauma such as being yanked out of the ground, peeled, cooked, and eaten.

3. What can you PROVE? Vegetables and plants initiate a massive hormone and chemical barrage internally when they suffer any kind of injury. This response is akin to the nerve response and endorphin release when

an animal is injured.

If I applied this T-K-P concept to the Solution Development stage of the distributed office output assessment process it might look like this:

STAGE: QUALIFY THE SOLUTION

1. Do I THINK the solution will deliver the expected benefits? Yes. The vendor's sales rep made the solution sound so good that I'm sure it will work as he described.

2. Do I KNOW the solution will deliver the expected benefits? Yes, because we installed the same solution at our Taiwan office and it delivered the same benefits that we have been promised.

3. Can I PROVE the solution will deliver the expected benefits? No, because we have not piloted or test marketed the solution at this customer's location. A pilot of the solution will give us the proof that the solution will (or will not) deliver the expected benefits for this company.

If the IT Manager in the above story of the executive presentation applied the Think, Know, Prove rigor to his assertion that his departments were not operating inefficiently, it would have *forced* him to be *honest* with himself and eventually understand that once he tried to *prove* his belief that things were operating efficiently, he would have come to the conclusion that he had a problem and should take action to address it.

- He *thought* his departments were operating efficiently

- He believed he *knew* things were going well because he never received any serious complaints from the user community

- However, he could not *prove* that his departments were operating efficiently, because he had not undergone any testing or other rigorous activity to gain that proof. And if he was honest with himself, he would realize that the only way he would *know for sure* is to do the diligence necessary to get that *proof.*

The Think, Know Prove Concept	
Think	This is fundamentally an opinion. Oftentimes, depending on the topic at hand, the opinion of an expert or other authority can give a company enough confidence to take an action. Otherwise, for the non-expert, when it comes to making significant decisions, who cares what you think?
Know	Knowledge can be the result of experience, and if a company or a person has had specific, relevant experiences with the exact (or very similar) problem under consideration, that experience (knowledge) can be useful and even sufficient in basing some decision on.
Prove	A proof of something almost always requires testing of a hypothesis, theory or piece of data for validation. It is not possible to prove everything, and sometimes the results from the testing of a hypothesis that was non-provable can be very useful and even better than general knowledge. But when combined with knowledge, a proof (or the test results of a hypothesis that could not be proven) can be even more credible.

PART THREE

DIAGNOSING THE PROBLEM

chapter nine
WHERE DO I BEGIN? (THE DISC)

THE FIRST STEP TOWARDS DIAGNOSING A PROBLEM is acknowledging that you might *have* a problem, and deciding that it's worth your while to put forth the effort necessary to clearly determine if, indeed, you do have a problem.

So, how do you know if your hardcopy environment is in need of an overhaul? Don't you fret; I'm gonna provide you with an easy way to determine whether or not you have paper problems. But for starters, here are a few considerations that comedian, Jeff Foxworthy (of "You might be a redneck" fame), might offer up:

"... YOU MIGHT HAVE A PAPER PROBLEM"

- If your vendor's copier service technician gets invited to your company's annual picnic because he's in the office so much that everyone assumed he was an employee, then you might have a paper problem

- If your desktop services manager answers, "Duplexing? What's that?" when you ask him or her about that specific feature, then you might have a paper problem

- If you still have an IBM Model 3800 laser printer and you're not a museum, then you might have a paper problem

- If you think your Hewlett-Packard LaserJet Model II printer is all the rage, then you might have a paper problem

- If you still *have* a Hewlett-Packard LaserJet Model II printer, then you might have a paper problem

- If your Facilities Manager has to go to Wikipedia.com to look up the definition of a "network," then you might have a paper problem

- If your users still wait for your fax machines to stamp that little red circle on the bottom corner of the fax pages they send, then you might have a paper problem

- If you notice a high percentage of end-users carrying large boxes marked "Best Buy" or "Staples" into their cubicles, then you might have a paper problem

- If your copier service technician has to be escorted to your copy room by armed security guards, then you might have a paper problem

- If your end-users have to call the helpdesk and ask: "Where are the rolls of thermal paper for the fax machines?" then you might have a paper problem

- If there is a piece or tape or a rubber band holding together any part of a printer in your building, then you might have a paper problem.

- If your company's official policy response to users who complain that they don't have adequate hardcopy functionality necessary to do their jobs is: "Piss off!", then you might have a paper problem

- If your end-users think the process for making copies on the copier is to: pull out a pair of latex gloves from the box that's sitting on the copy machine; open the front panel of the copier; hold your breath so that the flying toner particles don't get into your nostrils; pull out the jammed piece of paper; close the copier door; kick the copier; curse at it; make your copies; open the door again and remove the new jammed pieces of paper so that the copier is available for the next user — then you might have a paper problem.

And if these considerations don't convince you that your office output environment might be in need of attention, then maybe the questionnaire that follows in the next section will.

THE DOCUMENT-RELATED
INFORMATION SUPPLY CHAIN (DISC)

In November, 2003, I coined the term *Document-related Information Supply Cain* to formally describe the organizational processes related to information flow and paper output production. To provide a better understanding of the term and to put it into context, I offer the following definition:

THE INFORMATION SUPPLY CHAIN is the flow of information from point-to-point in the business process, within companies and between companies. The *Document-related Information Supply Chain* (DISC) is the information supply chain that involves the creation and production of documents at some point along the process. A "document" can be defined as: a written or printed paper providing information. So, the DISC is the flow of information that at some point involves paper.

THE DOCUMENT-RELATED INFORMATION SUPPLY CHAIN

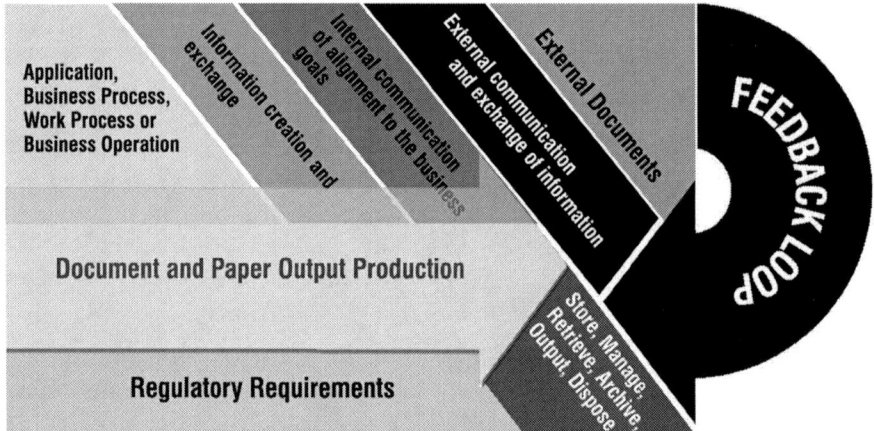

Tab Edwards, *The DISC Workshop, 2003*

In order to understand the magnitude of a company's paper problems, the company must first determine whether or not they actually *have* a problem, and if so, just how bad the problem is and if it's worth doing anything about in the short-term.

There are many ways that companies can gain detailed intelligence about their DISC and their distributed office output environment in general. Two that I will discuss herein are the *Document-related Information Supply Chain Planning Session* and the *Hardcopy Operational Analysis*.

THE DISC PLANNING SESSION FRAMEWORK

The easiest way for a company to determine if they have a problem of a magnitude that warrants corrective action, is to *understand* the area of consideration and determine how far the condition that exists in the environment deviates from (or provides an opportunity for) satisfying the company's (or the departments, the division's, etc.) business objectives. And some of the most effective ways that I have found to gain a thorough *understanding* of a company's DISC is by conducting a DISC planning session and performing a detailed analysis or assessment of the environment(s) of interest.

They say a picture is worth a thousand words, so I'm gonna forego writing a thousand-word description of the DISC Planning Session process, and instead, provide you with a picture that will explain it in a glance (below):

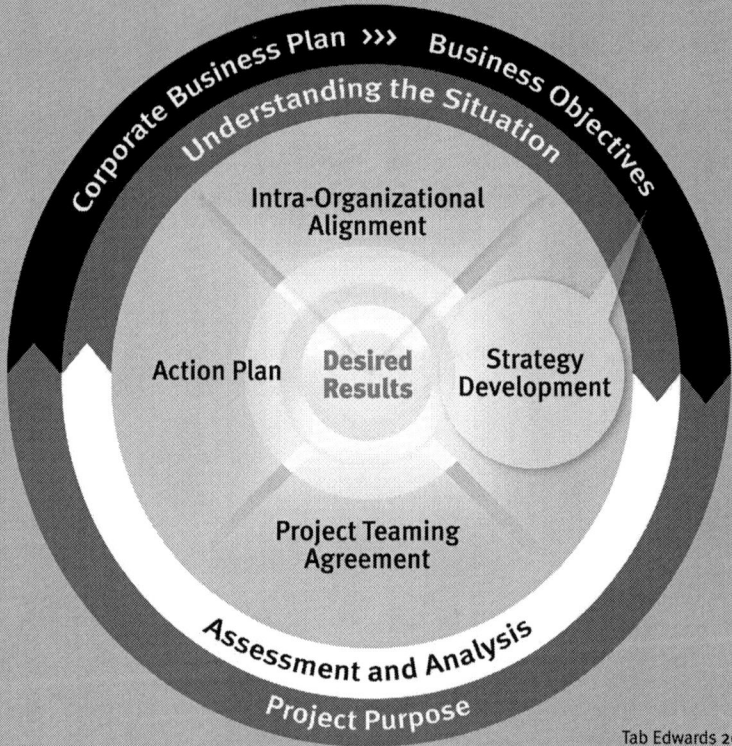

Document-related Information Supply Chain (DISC) Planning Session Framework

Corporate Business Plan >>> Business Objectives

Understanding the Situation

Intra-Organizational Alignment

Action Plan — Desired Results — Strategy Development

Project Teaming Agreement

Assessment and Analysis

Project Purpose

Tab Edwards 2003

Simply put, the DISC Planning Session is a methodology I developed to facilitate the development of "something" that will lead to an improvement of whatever DISC-related issue the company wants to explore. That "something" to which I refer can basically be anything. Whether the company wants to better understand what's going on in their DISC, develop a strategy (more on that later), review a workflow process, figure out what hidden problems may exist in the company, review a planned DISC-related project or application, bring alignment between different organizations within the company (e.g. IT and Facilities) and develop an organization structure for it, or if the company simply wants to check to see whether or not its departments are working towards the attainment of the company's business objectives, the DISC Planning Session framework can help.

I am providing the planning session framework here because the planning session is something that any manager with workshop facilitation skills can conduct for his or her company. The main things to consider when you conduct a DISC Planning Session are the following:

- **BUSINESS OBJECTIVES.** What are you trying to accomplish through the DISC planning session? How does that relate to (and support) the relevant business objectives?

- **PARTICIPANTS.** If progress is to be made, then the "right" audience must participate in the DISC workshop. Typical participants include (but are not limited to): The Chief Information Officer; Deputy CIO; Director-level managers from the relevant disciplines; Business Unit Manager; User Services Manager, Manager of Administration; Process-knowledegable user representative; Others at the customer's discretion.

- **BUY-IN AND SUPPORT.** All parties must agree that — whether they are 100% on-board with the ultimate team's decision or not — they will support the consensus built through the process.

THE DISC QUESTIONNAIRE

My recommended assessment & analysis methodologies will be described in detail later in the chapter, but for starters, here is a simple quiz that I give to clients when I perform DISC consulting engagements. This simple 20-question questionnaire can serve as the first step in determining if your distributed office output environment needs further attention.

THIS IS HOW IT WORKS: For each question you must select an answer of either "YES", "NO", or if you're not sure or you don't know, then select "??". Beneath each of these column headings there is a corresponding point total. In some cases you will see "N/A" (Not Applicable) which means that YOU CANNOT select "??" as your answer to that particular question. After you have answered each question and selected a point total for each question, you must then add the total number of points for each column and then add each column's point total to receive your **TOTAL** final score for the quiz. Once you know your total score, go to the "Score/Ranking" legend to see how you fared. The table below describes the score ranges.

SCORE (Point Total)	RANKING
0 to 49	Your DISC/distributed office output environment is probably in pretty good shape and is likely operating at a relatively efficient level.
50 to 99	Your DISC/distributed office output environment is likely operating at a level consistent with that of the average company, meaning that your company is operating at a relatively inefficient level and could benefit from operational and device-related infrastructural improvements.
100 to 150	Ha, ha, ha! You're kidding me, right! You've got problems.

#	QUESTION	YES	NO	??
1	Do you know within 20% the number of printers there are throughout the organization?	0	5	N/A
2	Do you know your current ratio of printers-to-users?	0	5	N/A
3	Do departmental users have budgets and authority which they can use to buy their own printers?	10	0	5
4	Do more than 25% of end-users have their own personal printers?	10	0	10
5	Do more than four different printer manufacturers have printers installed in your company?	5	0	5
6	Do at least 50% of your network printers and MFPs have "private print" capability?	0	5	5
7	Do you centrally and proactively manage your printer and copier/MFP eet?	0	5	5
8	Do your network office printers have finishing features (e.g. stapling)?	0	5	3
9	Are users at least 75% "productive" with their use of output devices (printers, copiers/MFP, fax)	0	5	5
10	Does the typical user follow the "print it - then copy it - then possibly fax it" process for output?	10	0	10
11	Do more than 75% of your copiers/MFPs have 11 x 17 (A3) format capability?	10	0	10
12	Do you have toner cartridges on-hand for products that are no longer in use?	10	0	5
13	Are at least 90% of your MFPs (digital copiers) connected to the network?	0	5	10
14	Do you lease copiers/MFPs for longer than 5-year terms?	10	0	5
15	Is more than 30% of your printer eet older than 5-years?	5	0	5
16	Are more than 30% of your help desk calls printer-related?	10	0	5
17	Do fax machines make up more than 1 out of 5 of your output devices (printers, copiers, faxes)	5	0	2
18	Have users been formally trained on the value and use of your MFPs?	0	5	5
19	Do you know within 20% how much your company spends on output TCO (not just h/w, toner, M/A)	0	10	N/A
20	Is there a document initiative in place to reduce paper and paper handling?	0	5	10
	SUBTOTALS			

TOTAL

67.

The key to taking this quiz is that you must be *totally honest* with yourself, and you can't be embarrassed by the fact that your answers to some of the questions are not what you hoped they would be.

GAIN SOME INSIGHT

Once you determine that you might be operating a distributed office output environment that needs to be improved upon, it is then time to gain more detailed intelligence about the environment in order to accomplish the following:

- **Identify the factors that detract from the company's ability to accomplish its business objectives.** Is the company spending too much money? Is the company wasting money? Is end-users' time being wasted on un-productive processes? Can business processes be completed more efficiently?

- **Gain an understanding of the magnitude of the problem in order to determine if the problems are worth fixing.** Is the company spending, wasting, or losing enough money for you to care? Are the existing inefficient workflow processes causing the company to lose out to our competitors? Are those inefficient processes hindering the company's ability to realize more revenue?

- **Identify specific areas of the environment that can be targeted for improvement** — improvements that will yield the most *bang-for-the-buck.*

- **Understand the elements of a strategy that will have to be developed in order to *right the ship.***

- **Develop a cohesive DISC strategy.** If a general project strategy has already been developed for the fact-finding endeavor, then this DISC strategy can be incorporated as a solution development activity.

chapter ten
THE DISC HARDCOPY OPERATIONAL ANALYSIS

WHY HAVE COMPANIES NOT TRADITIONALLY PERFORMED ANALYSES and developed solutions to the problems that may exist in their distributed office output environments? The most common reasons given by IT managers when asked this question are: *the lack of in-house expertise in conducting such an analysis*; and *printers are not that big of a problem for us.* Over the last handful of years, however, companies have begun to realize that millions of dollars are being wasted in the distributed office DISC, so the second reason is seldom given anymore. That leaves us with the primary reason why companies haven't performed analyses of their hardcopy environment: *the lack of in-house expertise.*

But fear not, comrades, in this section, I'm gonna share my methodology for performing a DISC — Hardcopy Operational Analysis that includes printing, copying, faxing, scanning and user workflow. Other names used throughout the industry for this type of analysis include: assessment; hardcopy assessment; printer study; copier study; output analysis; and output study. But whatever you elect to call it, in the end, they all are ways to provide companies with data and information that will allow them to make informed decisions.

THE HARDCOPY OPERATIONAL ANALYSIS (HOA) is a streamlined approach for understanding a company's document-related information supply chain, determining whether problems exist along the chain, (if so) understanding the scope of the problem(s), and developing a solution to address the problems. The HOA answers the questions:

- Does the company have a document-related or hardcopy problem in the distributed office?
- What are the problems and what is the magnitude of the problem?
- Why should the company care about the problems that were uncovered?
- How can the company begin to fix the problems?
- How can the manager get buy-in from executives to support an initiative to fix the problems?

STAGES OF THE DISC: HARDCOPY OPERATIONAL ANALYSIS PROCESS

The stages of the HOA process span the gamut from the development of an initial strategy for approaching the project, through selling the ultimate solution to upper-management in order to get approval for proceeding with the plan. The stages are listed below and summarized in the table below. Details of each stage of the HOA will follow thereafter.

Stages of the Hardcopy Operational Analysis Process

Stage of the HOA Process	Summary of the Stage	Maps to Six Sigma Stage
Develop an Initial Strategy	A strategy is a plan of action to guide the activities of the project team	NA
Determine the Representative Study Group	Should you study the entire company or a small representative subset of the company?	N/A
Data Gathering	Collect device data, qualitative, quantitative, and cost data. Automated or Manual?	Define
Develop a Topological Map	Show where the devices are physically located throughout the study group.	Define
Perform a Workflow Review	How do users use hardcopy devices in the course of doing their jobs? Identify inefficiency.	Define/Measure
Synthesize & Analyze the Data	Interpret the data. What does it mean? Should you care? Why or why not?	Measure/Analyze
Develop a Solution for Improvement	Once the problems have been clearly identified, what fixes them? How?	Improve
Build the Business Case	Build the business case for why upper-management should invest in your proposed solution.	D.M.A.I.C.

STAGE 1: DEVELOP AN INITIAL STRATEGY

Although it is not often necessary for the experienced consultant or manager to develop a detailed strategy when conducting the initial *Understanding the Situation* stage of a major improvement project, it could be useful in keeping everyone focused on the task at hand as well as making sure that all aspects of the engagement have been considered and planned for. These are the things that can make a project operate like clockwork. So, if you decide to develop a strategy for your project, read on ...

Before embarking on any project that will involve time, resources and even money, it's not such a bad idea to develop a strategy that will guide the activities of the project team and keep the team's efforts focused on those activities that will satisfy the objective of the task. But what exactly is a *strategy*, anyway? Different people have different definitions of what a *strategy* is. A strategy can be something complex or something embarrassingly simple. But if it helps you achieve your objectives in the most efficient manner, then it's a successful strategy. Consider:

A mechanical engineer and a 17-year-old high-school drop-out are standing on the edge of a lake wanting to get across to the other side. The lake is approximately 100-yards across and 22-feet deep at its deepest point. There are no boats, canoes, or other floatation devices available to them; they have only the natural materials available to them where they stand.

The engineer had it licked. He had developed a strategy that would surely get him across the lake. He decided that the best way to get across was to do the following:

▪ First, he would use some of the sharp-edged rocks as cutting instruments and cut the fallen tree branches into 6-foot-long pieces.

▪ He would then hollow out a tree limb, use a sharp rock to cut a hole in one of the maple trees, and insert the hollowed-out tree limb into the tree to extract sap.

- After that, he would rub two sticks together to create a fire (after all, every engineer was a boy scout at some point in their lives). He would use the fire to heat the sap which would then be used to bind the 6-foot long pieces of tree branch into a leak-proof raft. Ingenious!

- He would then wait for the lake to calm so that his ride across it would be peaceful.

The engineer estimated that — from start to finish — he would have his raft completed in approximately 4-hours. Almost bragging, the engineer asked the snotty-nosed punk drop-out how he planned to get across the lake. The kid replied, "I'm just gonna swim!"

What do the following things have in common?

- "My company will only purchase printers that are colored bright purple!"

- "Starting in January 2008, we will *purchase* all copiers and MFPs (as opposed to leasing them)."

- "On an ongoing basis, when each printer turns six-months old, we will replace it with a brand new model."

If you answered that they are all *questionable decisions* then you are only partly correct. These decisions could also be considered technology *strategies*.

STRATEGY DEFINED

WHAT EXACTLY IS A STRATEGY, ANYWAY? That is the central question: What exactly is a *Distributed Office Output / IT / Technology Strategy?* As I will try to illustrate through this section, a *technology strategy* can be just about anything you want it to be. By definition, a *strategy* is a plan of action; the art or skill of using *stratagems*. A *Stratagem* is a scheme for achieving an objective.

Within this definition lies what I believe to be the key descriptor of a robust technology strategy, namely: **A METHOD OF ACHIEVING AN OBJECTIVE.** Few companies anymore buy technology for technology's sake. Chief Information Officers don't buy the piece of *technology*, but instead, buy the *value* that the piece of technology will deliver. And if we agree with this assertion, then any strategy that is developed which focuses on *technology* should be re-developed with an emphasis on *delivering business value*, or — in other words — in support of a business plan and the achievement of some set of business objectives.

Okay. I know. That opens up a whole other set of issues. For instance, in the aforementioned example of the company that will only buy printers that are colored bright purple, they could have a bizarre business plan aimed at winning more business from the recording artist that-is once-again-known-as, Prince (in case you're unaware, he's into the whole *purple* thing).

If, indeed, this company is pursuing such a "strategy" for that reason, then they can make the argument that they have a relevant technology strategy because it's supporting a business objective of the company or business unit (to win more business). But to the outside world, would this technology strategy seem like a "good" one? Probably not, but the relevance of a technology strategy is not defined by what external influences say it should be, but is instead, defined by what your company believes the strategy should be based on — the *objective(s)* it is supporting.

A *technology strategy* is generally agreed to be a plan built around developing, implementing, maintaining, and exploiting a company's office technology assets (servers, applications, printers, copiers, MFPs, fax machines, scanners, etc.). It involves identifying technology priorities critical to the company's performance, while matching business needs (via its objectives) with that which technology companies have to offer.

General technology purchases made independent of a strategy typically don't support business objectives and needs. The slight improvements provided by the technology might deliver *some* benefits, true, but the technology won't live up to its full potential if not acquired, deployed, and managed as part of an overriding plan. Also, much technology purchased today may become obsolete just as a the benefits of a solution starts to kick-in This could lead to the technology "strategies" of the past — spend millions of dollars for equipment but figure out how to get it cheap!

A company's business activities are typically driven by the objectives of that company's *Business Plan*; this includes the company's technology initiatives. The IT organization should be an integral part of its company's business planning process, and therefore should develop their own plan to contribute to the achievement of the company's objectives.

My definition of a technology strategy is: *a plan of action to achieve business objectives*. And as such, the strategy defines how you will channel all of your resources and energy; any energy expended elsewhere is non-productive. A strategy also (often unintentionally) defines those things that a company should *not* do. Think about it. If you agree that a strategy is your roadmap or set of marching orders, then anything that you do outside of those guidelines does not support the attainment of the company's objectives, and is therefore wasted energy. So, by developing a clearly-defined technology strategy, any activities performed that are not in support of the strategy are things that you should probably not do.

SO HOW DO I DEVELOP A TECHNOLOGY STRATEGY? The answer: Any way you want. There is really no standard process for determining the way a technology strategy should be developed. Should it be broad or narrowly-focused? Should it be a short-term or long-term strategy? Should it contain competitive aspects or not? Should it be build on things you have done to date or should we start from scratch? Should it address organizational restructuring requirements or not? There's just no single way to slice it.

However, since the linkage between a company's business plan and the associated technology strategy plays such an important part in a company's success, most experts will agree that the technology strategy should be developed based on the objectives of the company business units that the IT organization is chartered with supporting.

A technology strategy should serve as a common blueprint for both business units and IT to work from — toward a company's vision and business goals. This blueprint then drives technology investments, infrastructure decisions, architecture, policy decisions, and any associated changes in processes and operations.

DEVELOPING A TECHNOLOGY STRATEGY

As I stated above, there is no single or "best" way to develop a technology strategy, however, there are some activities and approaches that experience has shown could lead to the development of a useful, effective technology strategy.

1. UNDERSTAND YOUR DIRECTION. Assess and gain a thorough understanding of the company's and/or business units' goals, business objectives, and needs (these should flow from the business objectives). The office output strategy should be aligned with the business strategy, and until you understand the objectives of the business strategy, you will not know in which direction you should be heading as you develop your strategy.

Some companies may not have a formal business strategy for you to align with, but that shouldn't stop you from identifying IT initiatives and projects that will provide value to the company and its business units. If you endeavor to better understand the business, its challenges and the issues it is facing, then you will be performing the activities that will keep your technology strategy development efforts in sync with the company's needs.

Understand that aligning IT with the business is not necessarily adapting your technology strategy to a "formal" company business plan. It's more about engaging in IT initiatives that *support* the businesses needs.

2. DEVELOP THE PROJECT PURPOSE. This could also be referred to as a type of business plan or even a business strategy to some regard. Probably the first thing that should be developed is the strategy development project's *Purpose.*

The Project Purpose will become the guiding principle that drives the activities of the project team(s). From the project's purpose should flow the specific, measurable goals and objectives of the project. Each goal should be supported by objectives that are measurable and time-specific. In some cases the business unit will have already developed a well-documented business plan that you can take advantage of. In such cases it is optional whether the IT manager chooses to develop a business plan as part of the strategy development initiative.

3. CREATE THE STRATEGY. Again, a strategy is a plan of action for achieving an objective. Let's say (simplistically) that the purpose of your IT strategy development initiative is to: *Provide quality services to your customers.* And one of the goals that you develop in support of that purpose is: *To improve delivery of services to those customers.* And let's say that an objective that you set in support of that goal is: *To decrease job turnaround time to 2-days, and to accomplish this by 12/31/09.*

Using this objective as a guide, you would then be able to engage your customers to understand their existing job processes in more detail, identify opportunities for improvement, and lay the foundation for the development of a technology-based plan of action that not only addresses the issues, but also leads to the attainment of the objective.

When the strategies-to-the-objectives are developed, it is then easier to determine the things you need and the things you have to do in order to deliver on the strategy, including (but not limited to):

- Determine staffing requirements
- Define reporting structures and approval processes
- Determine infrastructure, supporting structures, and technologies.

This is generally accomplished by activities such as:

— **Performing an assessment of your current environment:** Not only will you want to investigate ways to maximize the benefits of existing technology, but also ensure that any technology, supporting processes, and infrastructures selected will support current and future business needs and objectives.

— **Selecting the solution and determining the support needs:** As with any other technology-based decision, companies will determine which potential solutions (and even strategies to some extent) would yield the expected benefits most efficiently (cost, timeframe, usability, etc.). Basically companies want to identify those initiatives that will deliver the greatest return (value).

— **Implementing the solution:** Solutions should be implemented using an approach that ensures you achieve the specific, measurable goals defined by the business plan. Effective support and change management plans should also be considered to increase the odds of deriving the full value from a solution.

4. DEVELOP THE DESIGN PRINCIPLES. Once the strategies associated with the objectives are developed, it's usually a good opportunity to develop the principles that will guide the solution design process.

5. FORM THE PROJECT TEAM. I am a firm believer in the notion that a strategy development project team should include representation from the business unit(s) that will be affected by technology strategy.

The streets are littered with strategies that fail — not because they were bad strategies — but because of poor implementation. In terms of technology strategy development and implementation, people are more likely to support what they help to create. The best strategy available is of little value if it isn't implemented. Experience shows time and time again that implementation fails due to lack of understanding and "buy-in," not for lack of quality of the strategic ideas themselves.

Gaining buy-in starts by involving the affected parties in the business planning and/or strategy development process. The level of buy-in is correlated with the affected parties' engagement and involvement in the creation of a shared vision.

6. DEVELOP THE IMPLEMENTATION PLAN. To restate what I describe above, solutions should be implemented using an approach which ensures that you achieve the specific, measurable goals defined by the business plan. Effective support and change management plans should also be considered to increase the odds of deriving the full value from a solution.

7. BUILD THE BUSINESS CASE. A business case is a management proposition supporting an investment or procurement judgment. It supports the adoption of a specific solution by a specific organization. The business case is typically prepared for decision-makers in order to obtain project approval to proceed and/or to secure funding for proposed initiatives.

Generally speaking, a business case is a justification process that companies use for project selection. It provides the details of how delivering on the project in question will affect and contribute to the corporate business plan (strategy). [See the chapter: *Building the Business Case* for more details]

8. SELL THE STRATEGY. Selling the strategy could include gaining acceptance of and support for the strategy, gaining a commitment to the strategy, and gaining consensus within the organization.

"BUT THAT AIN'T WHAT *HE* SAID!"

I'm sure some readers will read this book and notice that it may differ from what others describe as "the way" to develop an office output or technology strategy. The reason is probably because there are so many definitions of what a technology strategy *is*. And I can't say that either one is "right" or "wrong," because that depends on the objectives that the strategy is designed to help achieve. My position is that in order to tell anyone what specific technology solutions or processes should be included in a company's technology strategy, you first have to have a clear understanding of the business plan that is driving the technology decisions being made.

Here's an example. Several months ago I read a report that attempted to tell its readers how to develop an output strategy (also known as an office output strategy, or hardcopy strategy, or printer strategy ...). Anyway, the writer stated something like: Your output strategy must include things such as a procurement solution, a fleet management solution, an output management infrastructure, and a fleet optimization review ...

Sure, these are the kinds of general recommendations that will usually yield some benefits to the company. And because of that, they are good things to do. But these are things that can be done in absence of aligning with business objectives, and because of that, they are not so much robust office output strategies as they are recommendations to streamline operations. These are the kinds of things that could be done and have no effect on the business' objectives, needs, or problems. And if that's true, then — to the business unit executive — they have little to no *value*.

These are the kinds of generally-agreed-upon activities that help provide efficiencies to the IT organization because it makes their lives easier when it comes to supporting their print, copy and fax environments. And if that is what the IT department is interested in doing, then they could save the time of developing a "strategy," and simply gather a bunch of best practices, rules-of-thumb, and general guidelines to accomplish those tasks.

I believe the first thing you should ask yourself when deciding to develop a technology strategy is: "What is it that I wish to accomplish with this strategy?" You might determine that a set of simple "strategies" (or guidelines as I refer to them) such as the ones listed above (e.g. "My company will only purchase personal computers that are colored bright purple!") will suffice. Or you might conclude that following some industry best practices will serve you well. If you ultimately do conclude that a robust technology strategy is what you want to develop, then hopefully, my ramblings here will offer some things to consider.

STAGE 2: DETERMINE THE REPRESENTATIVE STUDY GROUP

Several years ago when I first began studying and performing analyses of companies' office output environments, most companies were of the impression that in order to perform an assessment that would yield "valid" information (information that represented the company's actual usage and costs), it was necessary to study every office throughout the company. At that time, most consultants (and hardware manufacturers) charges a pretty-penny for their assessment services. I am aware of many consultants that charged upwards of $150 per-seat (user with a PC) for an office study or assessment. So, if a company wanted to hire the consultant to study a department that had 200 users in it, the fee would be $30,000 plus expenses. If a company wanted the consultant to study 1,000 users, the fee was $150,000, and so on. As you can imagine, this could be a very expensive proposition for large companies that wanted to have their whole company assessed. But at those expensive prices, they couldn't afford to have a whole company analyzed.

So, many consultants — including me — began explaining how by sampling a "representative" portion of the whole company, we could extrapolate the results and those results would be "reasonably" representative of the whole company's usage and cost characteristics. This was not a new concept; consulting and analytical firms have been using sampling and extrapolation methods since forever. Some of the main reasons why I recommend (and companies agree to use) sampling includes the following:

- **COST:** When consultants charge a fee for analysis services, it becomes too cost prohibitive for customers to have their whole company studied. For instance, at $100 per-seat, if a 50,000-user company wanted to have their whole company assessed, it would cost $5,000,000! That ain't gonna happen.

- **COMPLETION TIME:** Companies have analyses done so that they can use the data to make recommendations for improvement. Very large analyses can take several months — even more than a year — to complete. By that time, the data would likely be outdated (not 100% accurate), and the project would probably not be hot anymore. Customers want the results as quick as possible.

▪ **REASONABLE ACCURACY:** Even by studying every department of a large company, you will not get results that are 100% accurate. Several factors determine this, including time. If you are finishing a study a year later, chances are the data you collected at the beginning of the year has changed and is no longer valid. Therefore, the statistical accuracy of the study data will be something less than 100% — maybe 95% representative. In order to get study results that are 95% representative (95% confidence level), you can study a small representative percentage of the population and get the same level of confidence.

▪ **DIMINISHING RETURN:** Statistically speaking, there comes a point in a study where the increase in sample size begins to yield results that are not relatively more accurate. True, by studying 100% of a company, you are likely to get the most accurate results (less variability in the sample mean compared to the true mean), however, there is a point where the added accuracy is not significant enough to warrant the additional time, resources, and cost associated with studying the extra population. (See: Power vs. Sample Size graph below)

▪ **PREDICTIVE MODELING:** Normally, companies use this analysis data to spot common behaviors or characteristics about the population being studied that they can then use to make recommendations and/or decisions. *Predictive modeling* is a statistical sampling technique used to make generalizations about a larger population; it is not necessary to study an entire population to develop such a model (hence the name "predictive").

▪ **RESOURCES:** Companies have to assign resources to work with consultants on these analyses and assessments. Most companies don't want to tie-up their resources for up to a year on an output study.

- **POPULATION IS NOT AVAILABLE:** In many cases, the entire population to be studied may not be available.

In most situations in statistical analysis, you don't have access to an entire population of interest, either because the population is too large, can't (or is not willing to) be measured, or the analysis process is too expensive or time-consuming to allow more than a small segment of the population to be observed.

So what statisticians do is try to determine the percentage of the population necessary to study in order to yield results that are *statistically significant* (represent the whole population). The most common "significance level" used in statistical analysis is 95%, meaning that the assessment finding has a 95% chance of being true or *representative* of the average (mean) activity of the whole population. This is also referred to as the "confidence level."

With my assessment methodology, I use *probability sampling* which is commonly used to extrapolate results from a small sample to represent the larger population. As a subset, I use *stratified random sampling* since I study groups (of the whole) that have varying output usage characteristics, such as the finance department, human resources, etc.

Random sampling is used to prevent bias of the sample. With random sampling, you can assume that larger samples will better represent the variability in the population. As larger random (stratified) samples are taken, the variability of the sample fluctuates less. So you should strive to capture enough samples (e.g. different department types) so that the variability of the sample matches the variability of the population. That's why it's a good idea to make sure the output characteristics of the sample group are representative of the whole company.

In general, the larger the sample size, the smaller sampling error *tends* to be. If we want to make accurate decisions about output usage habits for example, we need to have a sample size large enough so that sampling error will tend to be *reasonably small.* If the sample is too small, there is not much point in gathering the data, because the results will tend to be too imprecise to be of much use. On the other hand, there is also a point of diminishing returns (as I mentioned above) beyond which increasing sample size provides little benefit. Once the sample size is "large enough" to produce a reasonable level of accuracy, making it larger simply wastes time and money. This is a statistical reality that's easily proven by something called *statistical power* which, in essence, says that the more accuracy (power) you want you can increase the sample size to get it, but after a point — to get an increase in "power" — the increase in sample size needed is disproportionately high and not worth it. This is illustrated in the diagram below:

POWER vs. SAMPLE SIZE

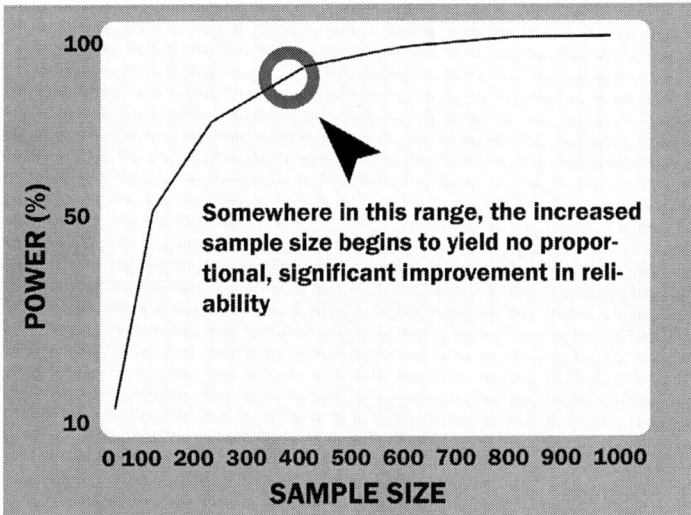

POWER (%)

Somewhere in this range, the increased sample size begins to yield no proportional, significant improvement in reliability

SAMPLE SIZE

As you can imagine, this is a very complex topic, but I'm simplifying it here.

When I perform studies and assessments, my objective is to find that sample size (percent of the population) to study so that the results are statistically significant (yield 95% confidence) and where it becomes relatively disadvantageous (in terms of time, cost, etc.) to sample larger than that population. For the type of studies I do, somewhere in the 7% to 15% range usually satisfies this objective based on *statistical power*.

There are many other ways to approximate the study group population size necessary to yield statistically-significant results. I have included a simple table that is relatively easy to use.

CAVEAT: The table below is intended to be used as one tool of many to help you and/or the consultant determine a study group size based on the objectives and requirements of your project. It is *not* intended to be used for determining the exact population size to study.

Calculating Sample Size and Margin of Error Table

Sample size for +/- 3%, +/- 5%, and +/- 10% Precision Levels Where Confidence Level is 95% and P = .5

Size of Population	Sample Size for Precision Levels		
	+/- 3%	+/- 5%	+/- 10%
500	A	222	83
600	A	240	86
700	A	255	88
800	A	267	89
900	A	277	90
1,000	A	286	91
2,000	714	333	95
3,000	811	353	97
4,000	870	364	98
5,000	909	370	98
6,000	938	375	98
7,000	959	378	99
8,000	976	381	99
9,000	989	383	99
10,000	1,000	385	99
15,000	1,034	390	100
20,000	1,053	392	100
25,000	1,064	394	100
50,000	1,087	397	100
100,000	1,099	398	100
100,000+	1,111	400	100

A - Assumption of normal approximation is poor (Yamane, 1967). The entire population should be sampled.

STAGE 3: DATA GATHERING

The most important stage of the HOA process could be the Data Gathering stage. Both the quantitative data (numbers-based) and qualitative data (operational, infrastructural, user-related, workflows, etc.) serve as the foundation upon which the entire assessment is built. The Data Gathering activity (or at least some portion of it) is normally performed on-site at the company's study group office location(s).

QUANTITATIVE DATA GATHERING:

The following types of quantitative data are typically collected during the data gathering activity:

- **THE NUMBER OF USERS IN THE STUDY ENVIRONMENT.** This becomes of value as you approximate the average annual cost of output-per-user. It also contributes to the determination of the *device-to-user ratio*. The device-to-user ratio describes the number of users — on average — that are using a single device. For instance, if a company has a printer-to-user ratio of 1-to-5, it means that each printer is supporting an average of 5 users. Although it is an indicator of the level of usage efficiency, this ratio, in and of itself, doesn't really tell you a whole lot; it must be combined with other data to paint a complete picture of device-usage (in)efficiency. And when this information is considered in light of additional findings, it can be valuable.

  A mistake that people often make is to apply an "industry standard" device-to-user ratio to the quantity of devices they place in the environment. Many IT managers have read various consulting reports that have, for instance, advised companies to deploy a "1-to-10" printer-to-user ratio in order to optimize their printer infrastructure. This doesn't really work. Sure, there will be occasions where this ratio is a good fit based on a company's usage and user requirements, but more often than not, it is a S.W.A.G. (Stupid Wild Ass Guess) rule of thumb. I have performed many assessments where printer-to-user ratios of 1-

to-2 were an "appropriate" fit for those companies based on the users' output demand. Were these companies operating efficiently? Usually not. However, if such companies tried to apply the generic 1-to-10 printer-to-user ratio, the ensuing chaos would have been frightening.

User data will also be useful in the workflow analysis and the *Time & Action* measurement. It will also help in the *Develop a Solution for Improvement* stage.

- **THE NUMBER OF PRINTERS, CONVENIENCE COPIERS (IF THE CRD IS BEING EXCLUDED FROM THE GENERAL OFFICE STUDY. ELSE, INCLUDE OTHER TYPES), FAX MACHINES AND SCANNERS – ALL BY MAKE, MODEL AND MANUFACTURER.** This information will give you a sense of the degree of excess capacity and waste that exists in the environment. It will also contribute to the determination of the device-to-user ratio. Another interesting thing that this data reveals is the number of different types of devices that are installed and the number of different manufacturers' equipment that is installed. This device data will also be used in the calculation of the Total Cost of Ownership.

- **THE AVERAGE NUMBER OF MONTHLY PAGES BEING PRODUCED ON EACH DEVICE (EX-CLUDING THE SCANNERS).** This data is the most important quantitative measure that can be collected during the data gathering activity. It serves as the foundation for device-usage (in)efficiency and cost-per-page. There are fundamentally two ways to gather quantitative device usage (pages produced) data: *Manually* and *Automated*.

AUTOMATED DATA COLLECTION

Many years ago when office output studies were coming into vogue, nearly every consultant and manufacturer that I can think of included automated device usage (page volume) data gathering software as part of their assessment methodology; I'm guilty, too. It worked like this: A company would hire a consultant or manufacturing company to perform an assessment of their distributed office output situation.

The consultant would install some usage tracking software on print servers and an agent on the users' PCs as a means of capturing the number of pages that were printed and copied (copier usage was also tracked using device-level hardware). The software would be used to track usage for some period of time — usually 30-days. After the 30-days of tracking usage, the data would be summarized, and the software would be de-installed. The month's worth of data that was tracked would be extrapolated (applied to a larger scope) to represent the average monthly volume or pages produced throughout the organization. To clarify: the month's worth of data that was collected was *assumed* to be an *accurate* representation of a *typical* month's output production.

Even today, some consultants still swear by this approach as yielding the most accurate monthly-usage data. I disagree. I spent many a loooong night teaching and tutoring MBA candidates on Quantitative Business Analysis (a.k.a. *Statistics*), and, one thing that experience had led me to understand was that — in my opinion — this data wasn't very statistically-representative of the "true" monthly average usage. Let's think about this for a minute: the assumption is that by using the software to track usage for 30-days (one month), you can use this data to accurately represent an average month's usage (paper output creation) throughout the company being studied. The logic goes that since *actual* usage was tracked — down to each device — the data is optimal because *actual* usage data is better than estimated data. Sure, I agree that actual data is better than estimated data. However, is *30-days worth of actual data* better than estimated data? Before I answer that question, let me first review the manual (estimated) data collection approach to page-usage approximation.

MANUAL DATA COLLECTION

It works like this: For each device in the study group, you collect the date the device was installed and the total number of pages that have been produced (printed, copied) on the device since installation. Then, you divide the total pages produced by the number of months the device has been in service; the resulting value will be an approximation of the average number of pages produced per-month on that device. And when added together with the other devices' data and extrapolated, you will have the average monthly number of pages produced through the environment.

The first question I usually get from customers when I explain this process is: "But how do you know when the device was installed? We don't keep such records for printers." Fair question. I, too, was faced with this dilemma several years ago when I developed a manual approach to approximate the average monthly page output per device. Then I found the answer: I noticed that the majority of printers manufactured have a *manufacture date* on them (or an actual *install date* on the printer configuration information page), and I thought that if I could find out the average amount of time that passes between when a manufacture date is applied to the printer and when that printer winds up in a company's office, I could *reasonably* approximate the install date for the printer.

So I asked some folks who work in printer manufacturing and distribution the following question: On average, how much time passes between the time you place a manufacture date on a printer and the printer ends up being shipped to a customer? Needless to say, this took some digging in a multiple locations. But eventually, the answer came back that an average of 2.2 months will pass for multi-user printers (those typically installed on the network and shared).

Being the methodical guy that I am, I tested this result against actual data. For some assessments I perform, companies will use asset management tools to track their hardware fleet — printers, too — so they will have actual install dates for their equipment. Whenever I come across such an environment, I collect both the actual install date *and* the manufacture date; then I compare the two to see just how reasonable and reflective my manually-collected data is of the actual data (usage based on the actual install date). And guess what. The *actual* install dates consistently show a 2-to-3 month difference (with an average of 2.4 months) between the manufacture date and the actual date of installation. This validates my assumption.

AUTOMATED DATA COLLECTION VS. MANUAL DATA COLLECTION

When consultants, manufacturers, and solution providers use print tracking software to determine a company's average monthly print volumes, we normally track printing for either 30 or 60-days. The question is: how do we know that the particular month's print activity that is tracked is reflective of that company's *actual* monthly print output?

If the company's print volumes fluctuate monthly (which most do), and we happen to track volumes during a "non-standard" print output month, then the extrapolated results could be wildly off. (INTERESTING TIDBIT: Over the course of 9-years that I have been performing office output assessments, my data shows that there are two months during the year — April and October — where the output volumes are relatively consistent with each other, and where their quantities are the most reflective of an overall *average* than any other months. What does that mean? Idunno. But it is intriguing).

Pardon the sidebar. Now back to our regularly-scheduled program ...

Consider the following example: Company ABC asks *Mr. Automated Software* and *Ms. Manual Collection* to each determine the company's average monthly printing volume. Mr. Automated installs print tracking software and tracks printing automatically for 30-days. Ms. Manual walks the floor and collects page volumes and install dates for each printer where possible. Let's assume that, by divine province, we know that Company ABC's actual monthly print volume is 10,808 pages-per-month as provided in the chart below.

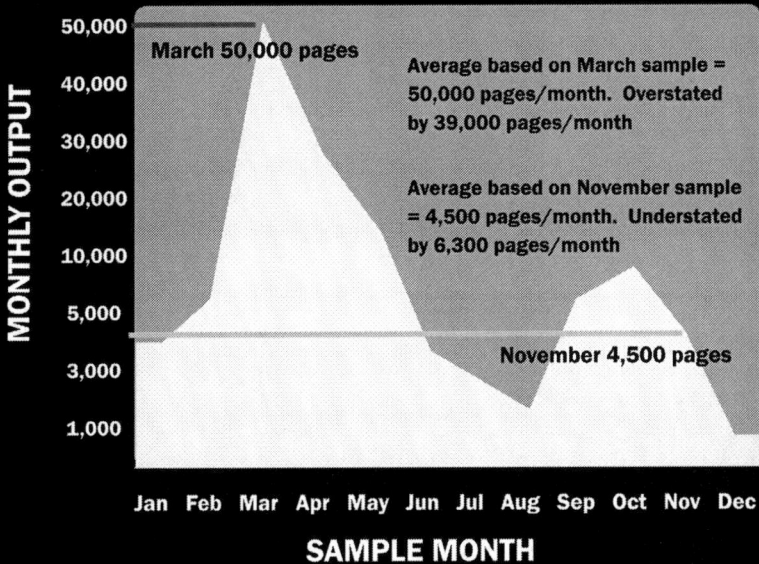

Sampling Error Based on 30-Day Sample

Actual average = 10,808 pages/month

March 50,000 pages

Average based on March sample = 50,000 pages/month. Overstated by 39,000 pages/month

Average based on November sample = 4,500 pages/month. Understated by 6,300 pages/month

November 4,500 pages

MONTHLY OUTPUT: 50,000 / 40,000 / 30,000 / 20,000 / 10,000 / 5,000 / 3,000 / 1,000

Jan Feb Mar Apr May Jun Jul Aug Sep Oct Nov Dec

SAMPLE MONTH

If Mr. Automated just so happens to track print output for the month of March and extrapolates that data to represent the full year, he would conclude that Company ABC's average monthly print volume is 50,000 pages, and the annual volume is 600,000 pages. This is obviously VERY overstated from the *actual* average of 10,808 pages per month.

The margin of error with this approach, in my opinion, is high because the same sampling error would exist regardless of which month he tracks — unless, of course, if he happens to track a month that *is* reflective of the true average (read: gets lucky), but he has no way of knowing which month that is — if indeed there *is* a month that is truly an average.

The problem with this approach is that the tracking period of 30-days (or even 60-days) is not long enough to yield representative results. Tracking software is intended to be used over time to spot trends and make informed decisions, and in that capacity, it is quite useful. However, it was not intended to be used for 30-day sampling studies.

Ms. Manual Collection, on the other hand, knows that in order to calculate the average or mean, she should add up all the data values (each month's output activity) and divide that sum by the number of data items (months = twelve). For example (and easy calculation), if Ms. Manual notes that a printer has been installed for 12 months and 12,000 pages have been printed on it, then the monthly average for that printer is 1,000 pages. She does this for each printer, adds them up, and divides by "N" (the total number of printers in the study group) to get an average monthly print volume at Company ABC. It can be argued that this approach yields results that are more reflective than Mr. Automated's results. Think about it. By the definition of an "average," Ms. Manual is determining the average monthly print volumes correctly.

As with anything mathematical, there is room for statistical error in each approach. For instance, with the automated approach, collecting data during a non-representative month will skew the page volumes used to represent the annual total number of pages. And with the manual approach, if a printer has been installed for 5-years, then the manu-ally-calculated average could be slightly off if we assume that printer usage decreases each year. However, the margin or error in Ms. Manual Collection's approach — I would argue — is more favorable than that of Mr. Automated's.

So, how accurate is each method of page output volume measure-ment? Let's consider the following:

AUTOMATED DATA COLLECTION. There are two calculations to determining the degree of accuracy of the data gathered using automated collec-tion tools over a 30-day (or 60-day) period. The first is calculating the probability that the *month* selected for the 30-day collection period is the month whose output production is representative of the average of all 12-months. The second is calculating the degree of accuracy of the resulting *data* in representing what the actual average monthly output production is.

There are 12-months in a year. We'll assume that the average month is 30-days long. And, contrary to what a few people may believe, compa-nies with traditional office environments rarely, if ever, print the same (or even approximately the same) number of pages each month; I have years of data to support this. Think about it logically: December (holi-days), January (holidays and New Year), February (short month), June, July, August (summer vacations), November (Thanksgiving). These events mean that there are fewer users in the office during the associ-ated months, which translates into fewer people producing printed and copied output, which means that output produced in these months will typically be less than a "standard" month where users are in the office for each of the 22 business days of the month.

So, what is the probability that by sampling paper output production for any one month (30-days), you will get a result that is equal to or representative of the average monthly output production of a full year? The answer: zero. Why? Because no companies' users produce the exact same number of pages every month. Okay, I'll be a little less strict with the calculation for this next scenario:

Let's assume that there actually *is* one month of the year whose user output production is about the same as would be the average monthly production of a full year. The problem is you don't know which month it is. So we pose the question: What is the probability of selecting one month out of twelve and selecting that one month that represents the average monthly output production? Using the formula for *Probability (P)* below, we can calculate the probability. There is a set of N elements (12 months) and a sub-set of n *favorable* elements (the one "correct" month), where n is less than or equal to N.

$$P = (n/N)$$

That means the probability of selecting the one month of the year where the user output production is an average of all twelve months is 1 out of 12 (8%). So, if there is only an 8% chance that the month you track is the "correct" month, that means there is a 92% chance that you will track an "incorrect" month.

The second part of the calculation is determining the degree of accuracy of the resulting 30-days worth of output production data in reflecting the true monthly average output production (i.e. the *Sample Mean*). The only way to perform this calculation is to know (or to be able to approximate) the actual average number of hardcopy (print, copy, fax) pages produced in a typical general office for every month of the year. This part can be difficult without any data to use as your frame of reference.

I have compiled data from the office output assessments I have performed over the years, and I have calculated the average number of pages printed per-month-per-printer — for each month of the calendar year — across all companies. These data support conventional wisdom that output production varies by month in the typical general office environment. I have also calculated the number of months where that specific month's print output production is within 5% (the margin of error that still leaves the data within a statistically significant confidence level of 95%) of the actual monthly average (mean). The result? Only one month's actual print output production was within 5% of the true mean (monthly average) of all twelve months' production; in other words, the probability that the 30-days worth of data collected using the automated collection software approach is within 5% of the actual monthly value is also only 8%.

The formula below can be used to determine the probability that both the "correct" month was selected *and* 30-day sample is within 5% of the actual monthly value. In other words:

- The probability of selecting the correct month to study = 1/12 or 8%

- The probability that the data you ultimately come back with is within 5% of the actual mean = 1/12 or 8%

Applying the formula:

$$P (X * Y)$$

$$P = (1/12) * (1/12) = 0.0064$$

In other words, the probability of getting a monthly output production value that is statistically significant (representative of the actual monthly output production volume in the environment with 95% confidence) using the 30-day automated data collection method is only .6% — or less than a 1% chance!

MANUAL DATA COLLECTION. As with the automated method, there are also two factors necessary to determining the degree of accuracy of the data gathered using the manual approach:

- The probability of the on-site install date being 2.2 months from the manufacture date of the device (as determined by the manufacture date stamped on the device or included in the device's configuration)

- The assumption that the *rate* of paper output produced in the general office decreases by the estimated average of 6%. (Although paper consumption increases each year, it is increasing at a *decreasing rate*, due to such factors as a decrease in the workforce and a move to digital solutions. Because of these factors most companies believe their overall printed and copied output rates go down slightly each year and, correctly, that their per-user consumption increases each year).

As described earlier, shared printers (departmental, workgroup, team-shared, etc.) and convenience copiers/MFPs are not typically manufactured and stored in warehouses or retail stores for long periods. In this era of technology manufacturing-on-demand and just-in-time inventory replenishment, manufacturers try to reduce the amount of time devices are stored in inventory (Inventory turnover rate. This is a common measure used to determine the cost effectiveness of a company's inventory and is calculated by dividing Cost of Goods Sold by Average Inventory — both are common financial statement values).

Taking a look at three of the top printer/MFP manufacturers in the U.S. — and calculating the average inventory turn of the three companies combined — my results show that the average inventory turn is 6.7 (the fewest turns were 4, which means that equipment is moved every 3-months on average). This means that, on average, each company moves devices from their inventory about 7 times per-year for all devices; and that means every 51 days (less than 2-months).

You will recall that my manual data gathering method assumes an average of about 2.2 months from the time a printer is manufactured until it arrives into a company's location. The calculation of *Average Inventory Turnover* supports this assumption based on actual manufacturer data. In addition, my own data from actual company assessments I performed where I compared actual printer installation dates (from asset management reports) to my 2.2-month-average estimate shows that my 2.2-month estimate is a very good predictor of the actual installation date.

Therefore, the probability that an estimate of the actual installation month can be determined using manufacturing dates can be calculated as follows: The range of months in inventory for a device is between 1.7 and 3-months; the average is 2.3 months. So, the probability that using an average installation date of 2.2 months from the manufacturing date is within 5% of the actual mean (average) of 2.3 is 100%. Now, if you're a purist, you will want to determine the probability — worst case. To do so, you will ask: What is the probability that choosing 2.2-months as the estimated installation date is statistically significant, given the actual measures of 1 month, 2 months, or 3 months? The answer would be P=1/3, or 33%. So, you can summarize by saying that the probability of my estimated 2.2-months-from-the-manufacture-date estimate is between 33% and 100% accurate; either way, this is far greater than the 8% (maximum) using automated software.

The second part of the manual method's accuracy calculation is the estimated rate-of-decrease in paper output production of 6% annually. My study data reveal that 42% of the printers in companies, on average, are 5-years old or older. Since 5-years (moving to 3-years) is the standard depreciable life of a printer, I will use this value in my calculation. My study data also reveal that the average number of pages-per-printer-per-month in companies, on average, is about 3,489 pages. If the rate of paper output production in the general office decreases by 6% annually, then the average monthly pages-per-printer values would be as follows:

Year 1:   3,920 pages

Year 2:   3,698 pages

Year 3:   3,489 pages

Year 4:   3,280 pages

Year 5:   3,083 pages

So, the probability that the average pages-per-device-per-month of 3,489 is within 5% of the actual mean (average) when taking into consideration the age of the device is 100%. In other words, the 6% rate of decrease in pages produced will not affect the average monthly pages-per-device using the manual data collection method because *this method already calculates the average using the correct formula for determining the true average:*

Average = (X1 + Xn/N) where "X" is the variable (e.g. the average monthly page values each year) and "N" is the number of observations (5 years in this example).

Comparing the Automated Software collection method to the Manual Data Collection method, we get the following:

Measure: The probability of getting a monthly output production value that is statistically significant (representative of the actual monthly output production volume in the environment with 95% confidence)

Automated Software Method	Automated Software Method	Manual Data Collection Method	Manual Data Collection Method
Best Case	Conservative	Best Case	Conservative
0.6%	0%	100%	33%

In addition to being what I believe to be a less-than-optimal sampling method, there are other issues with using tracking software at a customer site, including (but not limited to):

POTENTIAL DELAYS: In order for a 3rd party to install tracking software in a customer's environment, the customer will typically require a test of the application (for compatibility, viruses, etc. And there is a long list of known bugs in some print tracking software). This means that testing has to be scheduled with the IT Applications group. This could take days, weeks, or even months.

Consider the possibilities: By the time a customer tests the application (up to 30-days), schedules the install (2-weeks), tracks the data (30-60-days), and allows for problems (1-week), almost 3-months could have passed. In this time, manual data collection could have been performed and the entire study completed.

SECURITY: Today more than ever, customers are very reluctant to allow 3rd party software such as this to be installed on the network due to the heightened threat of viruses and system corruption. There are customers that won't allow it to be installed at all.

Final thought: Granted, neither the automated nor the manual collection approach is perfect; each has its flaws. However, when trying to determine the average monthly or annual page output volumes at a company, the simplest approach may indeed be the most accurate.

(QUANTITATIVE DATA GATHERING CONTINUED)

- **THE AGE OF THE DEVICES.** The age of the device is used to paint a picture of the level of inefficiency and fleet management & administration. Older devices use supplies and consumables less efficiently, they consume more power, the mean-time between failures decreases, they lack productivity-enhancing features, and they are often an indication of the degree to which the hardware fleet has been managed.

- **USER WORKFLOW TIME & ACTION MEASURES.** When performing an office output assessment it is critical to understand the user-related workflow processes. Not workflow from the standpoint of an *application* and how the *workflow* of the application progresses, but instead, workflow from the perspective of the user and how the user uses printers, copiers, fax machines and scanners in the course of doing their job. A workflow analysis will help you identify areas of user workflow inefficiency and identify where, in the use of hardcopy devices, users' time is being wasted and their jobs made more difficult.

Time & Action refers not only to the process users go through to create, retrieve, use, and return their paper output to their desk/ workplace (the *action*), but also the amount of *time* it takes to complete the action. For instance, does the typical user send a print job from his/her PC to a printer; walk to the printer to retrieve the print job; walk the print job to the copier to make stapled copies; walk the job to a fax machine to send it to another user; walk the job to the file cabinet for storage; then walk back to his/her desk? How long does that round-trip "wasting time walking paper" take?

The time measurement is taken (with a stop-watch) while walking the likely process users to through to complete the *action*. The amount of time required for users to complete the *action* can be converted to dollars (using an average loaded hourly-salary amount) which can be used as a *soft* dollar value in the financial analysis or business case development process.

- **COST DATA.** As mentioned in earlier, the company must ask itself: If we didn't have any printers, copiers/MFPs, fax machines, or scanners, which costs that we incur now would we no longer have to pay? The list should look something like this:
  - The purchase price or lease costs of the devices
  - The cost of paper
  - The cost of supplies and consumables
  - Maintenance costs
  - Power consumption costs
  - Phone line, port and per-call charges
  - Network port costs
  - Printer-related network management costs
  - Installation costs
  - Print servers and software license costs

- Helpdesk costs
- Asset management costs
- Floor space/real-estate costs
- Personnel costs/key operator costs
- User training costs
- Various productivity and soft costs
- etc ...

QUALITATIVE DATA GATHERING

The following types of quantitative are collected during a typical office output assessment.

- **USER FEEDBACK.** It is not enough to simply collect data about the devices and their associated costs, rather, it is almost equally important to collect feedback and input from the users of the devices. Admittedly, cost savings are what most companies ultimately want to achieve when undergoing an in-depth office output assessment. Unfortunately, in their zeal to save some bucks, many companies ignore the human factor of an optimization effort — *user be damned!* But how often have we heard of (or experienced) cases where a company implemented a cost-cutting solution that was ultimately rejected by the users and was, subsequently, relegated to the status of being "just another batch of hardware that no one uses to the fullest extent"?

  There are a handful of ways that user input and feedback can be included in the assessment process; the two most popular being the End User Interview and the User Questionnaire.

  Interviews and questionnaires are easy ways to gain an understanding of the things users like and dislike about the current hardcopy infrastructure and the associated usage processes. This feedback should be considered along with the quantitative data in order to form a complete picture of the ills of the current state environment. It should also be used in the solution-for-improvement effort.

- **USER WORKFLOW ACTION.** This was described in the previous section ("User Workflow Time & Action Measures") so I won't provide great detail in this section. The things to understand about device-related user workflow are how users use the devices in the course of performing their job functions, the things about those workflow processes that detract from the users' job-related productivity, and what the users need in order to become more productive as it relates to their use of hardcopy devices and the associated applications.

- **THE GENERAL ENVIRONMENTAL CONDITIONS:** Environmental conditions include those things about the physical environment that should be considered when developing solution options for improving the current state. This can include such things as: physical space limitations, power requirements, the ability to add a network drop if needed, dust, heating and cooling requirements, and safety-related issues. I have worked on projects where the solution that was initially designed to improve upon the current state environment could not be implemented because of such physical environmental characteristics and, therefore, had to be re-worked to accommodate the nuances of the location.

STAGE 4: DEVELOP A TOPOLOGICAL MAP

A physical topology (a floor plan/map showing the layout and the locations of the hardcopy devices on the floor being studied) can help when analyzing the user workflow processes as well as facilitate the design for improvement. It gives you a graphical representation of how the floor looks today, while serving as a tool to facilitate the explanation of how the floor's device-layout will look with the planned future state solution. But frankly, I got the most value from marking it up and using a paper copy of it to design the recommended future state solution.

STAGE 5: PERFORM A WORKFLOW REVIEW

THE USER WORKFLOW ACTION was described in the previous section ("User Workflow Time & Action Measures") so I won't provide great detail in this section. The things to understand about device-related user workflow are how users use the devices in the course of performing their job functions, the things about those workflow processes that detract from the users' job-related productivity, and what the users need in order to become more productive as it relates to their use of hardcopy devices and their associated applications.

When performing a user workflow analysis it is important to learn — from as many users as practical — the "typical" processes that users on the floor go through (when using printers, copiers, fax machines and copiers) in the course of getting their jobs done. How do you do this? One way is to ask this question in the user interviews and/or through the user questionnaires. Another approach is to start at each corner of the floor, identify the locations of the shared printers, copiers and fax machines, and walk the process of completing an output production and retrieval action — taking note of why users go through such processes in the workflow action. This process will give you a first-hand look at why user workflow processes are inefficient (if that is the case), and just how frustrating the workflow action is to the users.

STAGE 6:
SYNTHESIZE THE DATA AND ANALYZE THE ENVIRONMENT

Okay. You've collected all of this data, now what? Now it's time to put all of this stuff in order, scrub it, synthesize it, and use it to design a solution for improvements and build a business case to get funding approval to implement the proposed solution.

Consultants can spend weeks and even months analyzing the data that results from an office output assessment. Though I agree that slicing the data lots of ways can reveal some interesting information, I also believe that — based on what the company is trying to accomplish through the assessment process — a handful of key metrics can tell you all you need to know about the level of waste and inefficiency in an environment. At a minimum, I recommend analyzing the following metrics:

PRINT

- **THE AGE OF THE DEVICES** — specifically, the percentage of devices that are older than 3 and 5 years. Most companies still depreciate printers over 5 years using straight-line depreciation. This means the cost of the printer is equally spread over 5 years, and an equal dollar amount is applied to each year of the 5-year depreciable life. Some companies will *expense* printers that fall under a certain dollar amount, say $1,000. Any printer costing below this $1,000 threshold gets fully charged-off in the year of acquisition.

  As mentioned earlier, the age of the printers will give you an indication of the degree to which the print infrastructure is managed and administered. As a rule-of-thumb, if more than 25% of the printers in the study group are older than 5-years, chances are that the environment is incurring higher operating costs than necessary, the devices are not as reliable as they have been, there are a noticeable amount of user complaints, and the printers are not being bought and placed under the structure of any plan.

- **THE RATIO OF USERS-TO-DEVICES.** In and of themselves, user-to-devices ratios don't mean a whole lot. However, taken into consideration along with the other metrics listed here, they can complete a story. In general (assuming other data supports this finding), the lower the ratio, the more inefficient the printer infrastructure. Conversely, up to a point, the higher the ratio, the *more* efficient the infrastructure.

  For instance, studies across the Pharmaceutical industry shows that Pharma companies consistently show printer user-to-device ratios of

1-to-1, meaning that nearly every user has a printer; in this case, the ratio is a sign of inefficiency.

On the other end of the spectrum, manufacturing shop-floors typically have printer user-to-device ratios of 15-to-1, meaning that for every printer there are 15 users. This ratio is a relatively efficient one for a manufacturing shop floor. However, a 15-to-1 ratio in an Insurance company is probably a sign of disaster! But, as I stated earlier, user-to-device ratios must be reviewed in conjunction with other metrics in order to understand the whole story.

- **AVERAGE NUMBER OF PAGES PRINTED PER-PRINTER-PER-MONTH.** This is one of the best indicators of waste and excess capacity. My experiences revealed that the average shared (network-attached, non-personal) printer that is operating efficiently in an office environment prints somewhere between 4,500 and 7,500 pages-per-month. This assumes a mix of printers ranging from personal (non-shared) printers to higher-volume departmental printers.

If your study reveals that the number of pages printed per-printer-per-month is only 2,000 pages, then that is a good indication that there is excess printer capacity in the study group and that you probably have either too many printers and/or printers that are "too big" for the level of print demand in the environment. And if you find that the average number of printed pages per-printer-per-month is, say, 12,000 pages, then that's not necessarily a bad thing. You have to interpret this finding in light of other findings to determine whether it's favorable or not. For example, if you also find that the user-to-device ratio in this study group is 7-to-1, there are few user complaints, and the fleet is relatively new, then it could mean that you are running a high-performance print infrastructure. But if the ratio is 3-to-1 and the fleet is old, then maybe that 12,000 page-per-device average is high. Again, you must interpret all the data together in order to form a valid picture of how good or bad things are in the print environment.

One question I often get is: What is the "Duty Cycle" of a printer or copier/MFP, and, based on that, how many pages-per-month should a device print?

Basically, the *Duty Cycle* is a theoretical limit of the number of pages that can be printed on a printer or MFP, or copied on a copier each month, and not void any service warranties on the device. It does NOT mean that you should aim to print an amount of pages each month equal to the device's duty cycle. There may be a few exceptions, such as cases where the printers are dedicated devices cranking-out mainframe pages. But even in such cases I wouldn't recommend it.

If you plan on using the duty cycle to approximate the number of pages a device can be expected to realistically produce each month (in the general office), then I recommend setting a target page volume for a device at 3% to 10% of the device's monthly duty cycle. For instance, If a printer has a monthly duty cycle of 200,000 pages, then it's not a bad idea to shoot for printing between 6,000 and 20,000 pages-per-month on the device. Why? Lots of reasons, but the main one I believe is the *queuing* factor.

For example, if the average size of a print job is seven pages and the average user makes 3 trips to the printer daily, then each user will print 21-pages-per-day. That equates to 9,000 pages-per-day, which means that 432 users will print to that printer per day (ridiculous, ain't it?). And when you factor in toner changes, paper refills, supplies replenishment, paper jams, etc., it becomes easy to see how this would not work in an office environment.

The number of trips to the printer and the average size of a print job used in the example above are for illustration purposes only. Recent studies show that the average size of a print job is approximately 4.5 pages, and the average user prints about 4 times per day (Oxford Hill Consulting). Also, more than 2/3 of jobs printed consist of text only, and more than 90% are printed on 8.5" x 11" (A4) size paper.

- **THE PRECENTAGE OF PERSONAL PRINTERS.** Personal printers do have their place in the office. However, "too many" personal printers in the office could be pricey. If more than 1-in-5 (20%) of the printers in the study group is a personal printer, it could be an indication that the company is operating a higher—cost-than-necessary printer environment.

  On average, the total cost of owning and supporting a personal printer is higher than that of a networked printer that is shared (on a cost-per-page basis). Why? In general, it's due to scale and the number of pages produced on the respective printers. My data shows that users with personal printers — regardless of the size or model of the printer — print an average of between 288 and 340 pages-per-month on the device. If you take the annual total cost of ownership of the printer (taking into consideration the aforementioned TCO cost factors) divided the annual number of pages produced on the printer, the average cost-per-page will usually be higher than that of the shared printer. A key reason for this anomaly is the fact that users buy "inexpensive" ink-based color printers to use as their personal printers. The cost of consumables for such devices is higher than that of higher-volume toner or page-wide-array format printers. In addition, when users buy personal printers through their expense accounts or departmental budgets they invariably get them added to the company's break-fix support agreement where the annual cost to support these printers is more than the purchase price of the device.

- **THE TOTAL COST OF OWNERSHIP.** TCO is simply defined as the total cost of acquiring, owning and making an asset available to users over time. It is a true measure of what it *costs* to own a device. Excuse me for a minute, but there's a point I've just gotta make regarding TCO:

  Every day you see manufacturers touting the idea that their brand of printer "has a lower TCO than the competitors'". To fairly compare the TCO of different devices, you must first convert the TCO values into a common unit of measure; that unit of measure is *Cost-Per-Page.*

I've always been of the opinion that TCO in general, and cost-per-page (CPP) specifically, is something that can only truly be measured when a printer is being used in normal operation. Think about it: what are the main factors that go into the calculation of total-cost-of-ownership/ CPP?

—   The acquisition cost of the printer

—   The cost factors and cost elements

—   The number of pages produced on the printer

So, let's assume we have two competing printers: *Printer A* and *Printer B*. And let's also assume that each printer costs about the same amount to purchase and that they were purchased on the same date. In addition, each printer is installed in different companies (which means they have different TCO cost factors). For simplicity, let's say the only real difference between the two printers is the number of pages produced on each printer (see the diagram below)

CPP is the Relative Measure of Efficiency for TCO

Printer B Costs More but Has the Same TCO and a Lower CPP

Printer A: $5,000
($1,000 annually)

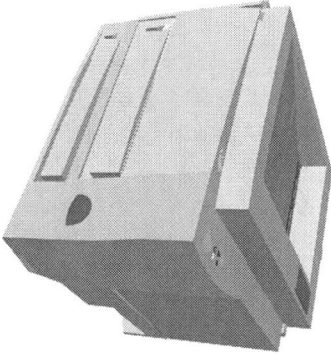

- Annual TCO Cost Factors = $600
- Annual Pages Printed = 30,000
- Annual TCO = $1,600
- **Cost-Per-Page = $0.053**

Printer B: $6,000
($1,200 annually)

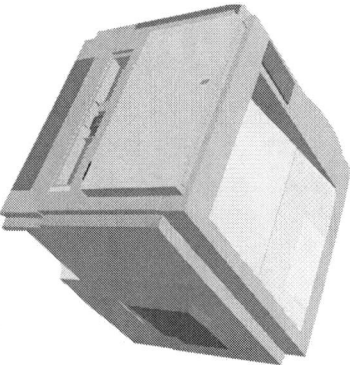

- Annual TCO Cost Factors = $400
- Annual Pages Printed = 52,000
- Annual TCO = $1,600
- **Cost-Per-Page = $0.031**

This example illustrates how it is possible for a higher-priced printer to have a lower cost-per-page. Two major factors influencing TCO/CPP are: (1) the environment in which the device is located (including the associated costs); and (2) how heavily the printer is being used. So, until you know how the device will be used in production and the environmental cost factors that will be applied to the printer (or copier or MFP), you cannot actually determine the TCO/CPP of the printer, and therefore, will not be able to perform a real-world comparison between competing devices. And if you can't do that, then you can't *really* say that when a company buys your printer it will have a lower TCO/CPP than the competitors'.

I know some of you printer and MFP manufacturers are saying: "Yeah, but the TCO and CPP comparisons we state assume that each printer is placed in the same environment, have all of the same costs, and produce the same number of pages every month. They are based on side-by-side comparisons in a lab setting." To which I say: Sure, but how often does THAT happen in the real world? Two-percent of the time, maybe? Never?

In the general office, people don't use printers and MFPs like that. Their output production can vary greatly from machine-to-machine, and the degree to which one department maintains their devices and uses them with care can be totally offset by another department's blatant abuse of the devices. These things will have an effect on the total cost of owning the devices and making them available (TCO), as well as the average cost-per-page of the pages produced on these devices.

- **THE AVERAGE COST-PER-PAGE (ACPP).** As described in the previous paragraph, Cost-per-page is calculated by dividing the TCO of a device by the number of pages produced on that device. It is a measure used primarily for comparison purposes. More and more, however, the *Average Cost-Per-Page* (ACPP) metric is being used by companies to determine the relative level of usage-efficiency in the device fleet. The average-cost-per-page is simply the average of the total population of

CPP results of a particular device category. For instance, the average cost-per-page for a company's printer fleet would be the sum of all of the individual CPP results for each printer divided by the number of printers.

As companies conduct office output studies and assessments, they are best served by calculating the average cost-per-page of *all* devices throughout the study group (printers, copiers/MFPs and fax machines combined), and the average cost-per-page of the printer fleet, copier/MFP fleet, and fax machine fleets individually.

The ACPP metric is very useful because, for instance, it can give you an at-a-glance view of just how (in)efficient the company's print, copy/MFP, fax and overall hardcopy environment is operating from a cost standpoint. If a company notices that the ACPP for its printer fleet is $0.10, and that the ACPP for its copier/MFP fleet is $0.08, then they can safely assume that there is an opportunity for improvement with both sets of fleets.

Some companies even use ACPP to identify and prioritize areas that require further investigation. For example, if a company uses copiers/MFPs from two different manufacturers, and, after performing an office output assessment, they notice that *Manufacturer A's* device fleet has an ACPP of $0.05 while *Manufacturer B's* fleet has an ACPP of $0.10, the company will want to investigate why one manufacturer's costs are twice as high as the other's — even though both sets of devices are being used in the same company.

COPY

In addition the metrics listed above, I also recommend that companies determine the following list of metrics for the copier and MFP fleet of devices in the environment:

- **% OF ON-GLASS 11" x 17" (A3) COPY CAPABILITY.** My study data shows that, on average, companies only produce about 9% of their copy/MFP output in 11" x 17"/A3 format. Some industry studies show that that number could even be as low as 3%. And still others, such as Gartner, suggest that this year, 2007, only 25% of copiers shipped in EMEA and the U.S. will print this format size.

What's interesting about this metric is that the majority of companies have a copier/MFP fleet of devices that is nearly 100% 11x17" equipped! When asked "why?" most companies respond by stating that "Our users say they need it," or "Our vendor sales rep recommends it," or even "Because that's what we've always purchased."

It's kinda like the "Boom-Box" example I use in some of my workshops. It goes like this: Your 16-year-old nephew has a birthday coming up and you want to buy him a nice gift. You are aware that his boom-box (portable stereo system) is broken and he really loved it. You check around, and you find a really fancy one that is complete with a CD player, a cassette player, and a radio (see below); it costs $249. Sure, there were less expensive ones available, but you wanted to get him the one with *the works*! Your budget for buying him a gift is $199, but he's a nice nephew so you decide to borrow the additional $50 so that you can buy him the system.

QUESTIONS I WOULD ASK:

- Was this an *effective* purchase? Why or why not?

- How will the nephew be using the boom-box?

- Why were the other boom-boxes much cheaper than this one? By how much?

I'll answer these questions in just a minute, but first I want to draw a parallel between the boom-box-buying uncle and the copier/MFP-buying manager.

- The uncle bought the boom box because his nephew loved his other one and this new one was just like it, but an upgrade. Oftentimes, managers, too, simply buy the newest, upgraded version of the copiers and MFPs they currently own (or lease, etc) just because it's newer and "better."

- The uncle bought a boom-box with a cassette player on it, even though only 1 or 2% of new music is produced on that format anymore, and more importantly, no teenagers use cassettes! If the uncle has asked his nephew or took the time to look at his nephew's music collection, he would have discovered this fact.

    The copier/MFP-buying manager does a version of this as well. The research shows that a very small percentage of copiers/MFPs are being used to create A3 (11" x 17") format output — especially on-glass copies. Yet, the manager continues to buy new equipment with 11" x 17" flatbed copy capability. If the manager had surveyed the users or performed a thorough assessment he/she would have found that, indeed, there is not a requirement for a complete fleet of A3-format devices.

Now, back to the questions:

- **Was this an *effective* purchase?** No, because it is overkill based on the requirements of the user (the nephew). In addition, the uncle could have saved some money by buying the boom-box without the cassette player included.

- **How will the nephew be using the boom-box?** For playing CDs and listening to the radio only. In fact, if the uncle did his homework, he might have found out the nephew's use of CDs and radio is rapidly decreasing in favor of portable music players like the iPod. Armed with this information, the uncle would have been wise to change his purchase decision altogether to something that was more practical and which had a longer shelf-life.

- **Why were the other boom-boxes much cheaper than this one?** The other boom-boxes were less expensive because they only contained a CD player and a radio. By how much? Who knows, buy I'm sure the uncle would not have had to borrow any money to pay for it.

This simple little example is used to illustrate what I have found to be a reality among many companies — they buy what they buy more so out of habit and because the *new thing* must be *better* than their current thing … uhh … because it's *new*, rather than buying copiers and MFPs (and even printers and fax machines) based on what's *known* to be needed. Ask yourself:

- Why change anything?
- What happened to prompt a change?
- What's broken? How do I *know* it's broken?
- Why do I need to buy something *now*.
- How do I know what to buy?
- Why am I buying the type and format of equipment that I am considering? Based on what information? How did I come by this information? Is it valid?

You may find that answering these questions honestly will help your company make better, more informed decisions that match the requirements of the user community, while saving the copany a lot of money in the process.

- **% OF COPIERS/MFPs ATTACHED TO THE NETWORK.** Although not as much of an issue as it has been in the past, the fact that companies still buy analog copiers (because they're *cheap*. Shame on you!) and MFPs — and can't/don't install them on the network is quite inefficient. Everyone acknowledges that analog copiers can't be installed on the network, and the only reason they still exist is because companies can get them for nearly nothing (*users be damned!*). So these devices are purchased with the full expectation that they will only serve as stand-alone single-function copiers.

MFPs, on the other hand, deliver their value by serving as multi-functional devices that allow users to complete their output production transactions from their desks. When MFPs are acquired and not installed on the network, you have effectively purchased a single-function copier; that's wasteful.

The reality is that this is still happening at most companies in varying degrees. I actually worked with a company that had only installed less than 50% of their recently-acquired (within 2 years) MFPs on the network. Yet, another company I worked with had installed over 95% of their MFPs on the network.

Why does this happen? Well, there are several reasons which I won't elaborate too much on in this book (you can gain additional insight in the chapter entitled: *Fragmentation*). However, I will say that one of the more common reasons is the struggle between the division that manages the printers (typically the IT organization) and the division that manages copiers (typically the Real Estate/Facilities, Purchasing, and Procurement organizations).

When MFPs came onto the scene in the late '90s, companies found themselves facing an interesting dilemma: where should the responsibility for ownership and support rest for these devices? After all, MFPs are network printers because users can print pages to them directly from their desks, and MFPs are copiers, too, because users can use them to create on-glass convenience copies. In addition, MFPs are sold by companies that both the IT and Facilities/Purchasing staffs have traditionally dealt with to buy printers and copiers respectively.

So what happens? Traditional copier manufacturers sold MFPs to the Facilities group and had to lobby the IT department to install them on the network. Depending on the backlog of IT projects, the installation of the MFPs often never happened. And don't be surprised to know that some IT departments get offended when they are "forced" to install things on "their" network that they had not planned for. In those cases, it's not hard to imagine how getting that MFP on the network will happen "when I (the IT manager) feel like it!"

FAX

In addition to many of the metrics described above, it is important to know the ACPP for faxed pages, and the percentage of fax machines as a percentage of all devices (printers + copiers/MFPs + fax machines).

- **AVERAGE COST-PER-PAGE FOR FAX.** On average, the cost-per-fax page sent or received is by far greater than that of printing and copying. Why? Because the cost of analog faxing includes phone line charges, port charges, long-distance and international per-call charges, and the cost of the device and supplies & consumables. These relatively high costs must be spread over the relatively small number of pages sent and received. It is not unreasonable to find the cost-per-fax page of $1.00 or more.

- **FAX MACHINES AS A PERCENTAGE OF ALL DEVICES.** This metric provides one of the easiest ways to determine whether or not you have "too many" fax machines in the environment. For starters, how many fax machines are "too many"? It depends. Analog faxing still does have a place in the business office for obvious reasons, including the fact that if the network goes down, you can still communicate via the analog fax machine. But as more ad more companies migrate to alternate, digital "fax" solutions, the number of stand-alone analog fax machines needed in the office continues to decrease.

The best way to determine the number of fax machines needed is through an assessment or a simple study of the faxing environment. But, from experience, I do know that 50% of the fleet (1 out of every two hardcopy devices) is too many. I also know that 1% (1 out of every one hundred hardcopy devices) is too few. The number that seems to provide good balance is somewhere between 5% and 15% depending on the functional area where the fax machines are being used.

- **ADDITIONAL METRICS.** There are many additional metrics and other helpful information that are uncovered during the course of a detailed assessment that contribute to a greater understanding of the environment, including such things as:

    - The number of different manufacturers whose equipment (by category) is represented in the study group
    - The pervasiveness of duplexing (2-sided printing)
    - The number of different models of printers and copiers/MFPs
    - The availability of convenience copying available throughout the department (not just in copy rooms)
    - The percentage of color and monochrome devices
    - The average cost-per-page for color printing
    - Device features and functions
    - Percentage of pages produced by type and size
    - The types (and quantities) of pages produced on MFPs

DATA INTERPRETATION AND ANALYSIS

The easiest way to synthesize and crunch all of the data that you gathered during the data gathering activity is to create a spreadsheet (or use some other tool) that will allow you to crunch that data and calculate the various quantitative metrics repeatedly. Some of the TCO cost elements require somewhat complex formulas to calculate, such as the *IT Management* costs which can include print server costs, licensing costs, application costs, IP connectivity charges, etc. And once you have applied all of the relevant TCO element costs and quantitative data to each device inventoried during the data -gathering stage, you will ultimately end up with a spreadsheet that looks something like the table below:

Monthly Costs	(Dummy Values For Example Only)													
DEVICE	PGS/ MO	TONER	SUP- PLIES	PAPER	POWER	ASSET MGMT	PURCH	SPACE	IT MGMT	HELP DESK	PHONE	DEPRE- CIATION, FINANCE	MONTHLY TCO	CPP
Acme printer Model A	12,603	$0.01	$0.00	$0.00	$0.00	$90.00	$34.50	$0.00	$535.07	$175.00	$0.00	$490.15	$3,607.08	$0.02
Acme Printer Model B	1,933	$0.01	$0.00	$0.00	$0.00	$90.00	$34.50	$0.00	$535.07	$175.00	$0.00	$163.38	$1,460.59	$0.06
Acme printer Model C	1,680	$0.01	$0.00	$0.00	$0.00	$90.00	$34.50	$0.00	$535.07	$175.00	$0.00	$300.00	$1,619.00	$0.08
ABC MFP Model 1	509	$0.01	$0.00	$0.00	$0.00	$90.00	$34.50	$0.00	$535.07	$175.00	$30.00	$593.33	$1,668.80	$0.27
ABC MFP Model 2	7,486	$0.01	$0.00	$0.00	$0.00	$90.00	$34.50	$0.00	$535.07	$175.00	$30.00	$416.66	$2,943.09	$0.03
XYZ Copier Model A	3,353	$0.01	$0.00	$0.00	$0.00	$90.00	$34.50	$0.00	$535.07	$175.00	$0.00	$500.00	$2,166.92	$0.05

And after all of the quantitative data from the data gathering effort has been crunched and summarized (as in the Table below) you will then be able to perform an analysis of the data. NOTE: The table below shows the industry average values from actual assessments across many industries that I have performed in recent years. It is being provided as an example of the types of summary metrics that can be assembled from the data gathered during an assessment.

Industry Averages	Averages	Generally Efficient (Range)*
Print		
· Age 5-yrs or older	42%	20% - 25%
· User-to-Printer ratio	4-to-1	7-to-1, to 12-to-1
· Average monthly pages/printer	3,489	4,500 to 7,500
· Duplex availability	29%	75% to 100%
· Personal (non-shared) printers	46%	5% to 20%
· Average Cost-Per-Page	$0.065	$0.025 to $0.04
Copy		
· Average pages/copier-MFD/month	8,745	12,000 to 20,000
· On-glass 11 x 17 capability	100%	25% to 40%
· User-to-Copier/MFD ratio	37-to-1	10-to 1, to 25-to-1
· Average Cost-Per-Page	$0.049	$0.02 to $0.033
· % of devices connected to the network	84%	90% to 100%
Fax		
· Ratio of users to fax machines	27-to-1	30 to 1, to 40-to-1
· Fax machines as a % of all devices (PCF)	25%	5% to 10%
· Average fax cost-per-page	$0.62	$0.25 to $0.33

* Guidelines based on assessment results and my experience. The degree of efficiency in these categories will vary between companies, depending on usage characteristics, element costs, and other such factors.

+ Some TCO calculations varied slightly between assessment engagements due to an inconsistency in the variables that different companies elected to include in the studies.

PART FOUR

TOWARDS FIXING THE PROBLEM

STAGE 7: DEVELOP A SOLUTION FOR IMPROVEMENT

The distributed office output solution development process involves:

- Understanding why certain assessment findings are "problems"
- Understanding what actions will fix the problems
- Determining the potential benefits of the fixes
- Mapping out how the "fixed" environment will look and how much it will cost (TCO). This is the solution.
- Determining the financial and qualitative benefits of the mapped solution
- Aligning the expected benefits of the solution to the objectives of the project
- Determining whether the Business Case for the proposed solution satisfies the requirements imposed by the company.

Below are some suggestions on how to interpret the assessment findings and use the information in your solution development efforts.

NUMBER OF USERS IN THE STUDY GROUP

The number of users included in the study group is the primary factor used in determining the quantity of people necessary to yield statistically significant results that can be extrapolated to the larger (non-study group) population in the company. If the number of users in the study group are too few, then the results of the assessment of that study group will likely be too few to yield results that can be used reliably.

Also, when developing the solution for improvement, the number of users can be considered when determining whether or not the resulting user-to-device ratio is an efficient one for the environment.

NUMBER OF DEVICES

The number of printers, copiers and fax machines in the study group serve as the foundation on which costs are applied to determine TCO (and subsequently CPP), and user-to-device ratios.

If your study results show that there are far more devices in the environment than are necessary to support the users' workflow processes and the page output requirements, then you should consider right-sizing the device fleet until there is a balance between user workflow efficiency (and functionality/feature requirements), page output volume requirements, and cost.

AGE OF THE DEVICES

The average age of the device fleet gives you an indication of how effectively the environment is being managed and administered. Older devices use supplies and consumables less efficiently. In addition, the mean-time-between-failures decreases; the result is a higher-cost environment.

Many companies are starting to depreciate technology hardware over 3-years instead of the traditional 5-years. However, I haven't really noticed a trend where these companies are replacing devices any more frequently than in the past.

Let's face it, devices are more reliable these days and remain operational (at a high level) for longer periods of time. So, if a device provides the features and functionality required by the users, if a device operates super reliably (with preventative maintenance), and if the TCO of the device is at a level that you're comfortable with, then it's hard to make an argument for replacing it. if, on the other hand, these conditions do not apply, then ...

WORKFLOW TIME & ACTION MEASURES

When performing a user workflow analysis, it's not enough to just track how users use hardcopy devices in the course of getting their jobs done, it is also important to approximate the amount of time it takes for the typical user to create, produce/print, perform a document-related workflow task, and return to his or her desk.

This Time & Action measure will give you insight into the likely degree of effectiveness of your planned solution at reducing the amount of time it takes the user to perform document-related workflow tasks. It will also help you zero-in on a specific aspect of the workflow process that is most inefficient from a time-waste standpoint.

USER FEEDBACK

This is where you hear it straight-from-the users'-mouths. Gathering data and performing workflow and Time & Action studies will only give you part of the picture. It is important to find out from the users what works and what needs improvement.

Also, it is important to get the user community involved in the assessment/solution design process to increase the odds that that you get their buy-in on any solution that you ultimately wish to implement.

USER WORKFLOW ACTION

What is the typical document-related work process that users go through in the course of doing heir jobs? How much of their effort is wasted "walking paper"? A user workflow action analysis will help you answer these questions.

I believe it is also important to perform a similar workflow action analysis during the pilot, trial and/or actual solution implementation phase of the project to determine whether or not — from a workflow standpoint — your (proposed) solution will providing the expected efficiency gains to the user community.

ENVIRONMENTAL CONDITIONS

When performing assessments, I sometimes come across offices that are quite old and were built eons ago. The most common places are colleges/ universities, hospitals, and public-sector locations. The challenge in such locations is making sure that the solution you design can be accommodated by the environment.

For example, some older locations have not been upgraded with adequate climate controls, network infrastructure or power outlets. Also, many of these locations are space-constrained, which can make it more difficult to design a solution for.

It is also important to keep in mind that the cost for any upgrades that would be necessary to accommodate your solution have to be included in your financial analysis.

TOPOLOGICAL MAP

Mapping the physical location of each device and the locations of the users on a particular   oor will serve as an excellent tool for visually spotting potential inefficiencies. For example, if you look at a completed floor map and you notice a cluster of 5 printers in a row in a mail room — next to a copier and fax machine — then you can easily identify that graphical representation as an area to investigate further.

A completed floor map also helps when designing a solution for improvement.

RATIO OF USERS-TO-DEVICES

In and of themselves, user-to-device ratios don't tell you a whole lot. Their value comes when you combine these ratios with other findings to form a more complete picture of what's really going on in the study group.

I'm not a big fan of applying a generic user-to-device target to offices without the benefit of having performed some degree of analysis. The reason is because, more often than not, you will be implementing a solution that is an inappropriate fit between what you are installing and what users require.

There are, however, some user-to-device ratio levels that are obviously outa whack. For instance, if you find that your office has a user-to-device ratio of 1-to-1, or 55-to-1, then it doesn't take Kant to understand that you've got paper problems.

AVERAGE PAGES-PER-MONTH

I find this to be probably the most useful of all metrics because this metric will instantly give you a feel for how inefficiently your hardcopy fleet of devices is operating (assuming you have a feel for the number of pages certain classes of devices should be producing in an "efficient" environment).

If I notice that the average number of pages-per-copier/MFP-per-month in a study group is 6,000, then I can immediately infer that their copier/MFP fleet is being underutilized by 100% — based on experience. And if I notice that the average pages-per-month-per-printer is 2,500 pages, then I can also infer that this study group has paper problems.

When designing a solution for improvement, it's always a good idea to calculate the average pages-per-device-per-month — both in the current and future states — so that you can determine up-front how efficiently your future state solution will likely operate.

PERCENTAGE OF PERSONAL PRINTERS

The percentage of personal printers in the environment is an indication of the level of management, responsiveness, and control in the environment.

More that 20% personal printers (of the total printer fleet) is a red flag that users' requirements are not being met by IT, there is a higher-than-necessary cost of operation, and/or that the device fleet is not being effectively managed and controlled. Is this rule of thumb cast-in-stone? Of course not. But is usually a pretty accurate indicator.

And what if a high percentage of personal devices is by-design? That's fine. None of the guidelines I'm providing herein are the gospel. It's just something that my experience has shown is worth keeping an eye on. See the next section on Personal Printer Guidelines.

TOTAL COST OF OWNERSHIP

Ultimately, when analyzing the hardcopy environment, managers are looking for opportunities to cut costs and save money. The true measure of what it costs to own devices and make them available to users is the Total Cost of Ownership.

When calculating TCO, it is important to take into consideration all of the relevant costs of operating your hardcopy environment. An easy way to generate a list of such costs is by asking yourself : *If we didn't have any printers, copiers, or fax machines, which costs that we incur today would we no longer have to pay?*

AVERAGE COST-PER-PAGE

Calculating the ACPP is the best way to calculate how much more costly (relatively) one device is over another. As illustrated above, two devices that have the same purchase price can have wildly different costs-per-page due to environmental cost elements and usage.

Don't buy into the notion that one manufacturer's device is *inherently* less costly to own than another manufacturer's device on average (as compared by ACPP). I can point to numerous examples where this is not the case. What's important — regardless of which technology you buy — is that you are maximizing the benefit of the device and avoiding excess capacity; that results in a high cost-per-page.

PERCENTAGE OF ON-GLASS 11" X 17"/A3

The question: Why purchase 100 MFPs with 11" x 17" on-glass copy capability when only 9 are needed? Studies show (mine included) that the typical company produces between 3% to 9% of A3-sized pages on copiers and MFPs. Yet, companies continually refresh their copier/MFP fleet with 100% of the devices having this feature. That is an easy opportunity to cut your costs of hardware in half by simply ordering fewer of that format device.

That is why it is important to understand usage characteristics in the environment. If users actually "need" that size format in 100% of the cases, then, fine, buy it. But if they don't, then use the opportunity to right-size the device capacity.

PERCENTAGE OF MFPS ON THE NETWORK

Simply put: Every MFP you buy today should be installed on the network. Period. Otherwise, you're paying for an awfully expensive single-function copier.

FAX MACHINES AS A % OF ALL DEVICES

Fax machines still (and will continue to) have a place in the office. Users know how to use them and they are reliable in the event of a network crash. The question is: how *much* of a place do they have in the office?

If 20% or more of your total devices are analog fax machines, then my guess is that you have too many based on what is the typical requirement for analog faxing. And if you conduct a study and find that you *need* 20% or more of the devices to be fax machines, then you've got other workflow-related paper problems.

NUMBER OF DIFFERENT MANUFACTURERS

The fewer the better. I have performed office studies where some companies had more than seven different manufacturers' printers installed. This is a problem for lots of reasons, including (but not limited to) user training, and the inability to standardize on supplies & consumables, and take advantage of discounts. Also, wasted toner cartridges seem to be a by-product of multi-vendor device fleets.

Think about it: a company like this probably has at least 8 different models of each manufacturer's printer installed. Multiply that by the 7 manufacturers, and you find yourself with 56 different models of printers.

PERVASIVENESS OF DUPLEXING

Duplexing (2-sided printing/copying) is an opportunity for companies to cut paper costs. Many older devices lack this feature. A reality is that, although you may provide a fleet that is 100% duplex-capable, don't expect any more than between 20% and 30% of users to use it consistently. Education and training are required to increase adoption.

NUMBER OF DIFFERENT MODELS OF PRINTERS AND COPIERS

See: *Number of Different Manufacturers* above

AVAILABILITY CONVENIENCE COPYING

In the old days, companies would install one, maybe two copiers in each office — at each end of the floor. Users invariably had to walk unproductive distances just to make copies and return to their desks.

Today, users who need on-glass copy capability don't want to (nor should they have to) walk great distances to get it. One of the promises of small MFPs is that they can be placed throughout the office and give users the convenience copy they need.

% OF COLOR AND MONOCHROME DEVICES

When calculating TCO, it is a good idea to calculate how much the company is spending on color copying and if the users are really *using* it. Page totals by device go a long way towards facilitating this calculation. But if you want to get more precise, you should approximate the amount of color coverage vs. monochrome coverage on a typical color (produced on a color device) page.

The use of color is becoming more pervasive in the office, and as the cost of color printers and supplies continues to fall, companies are buying them in greater volume. The challenge is to determine the average pages produced per-month-per-color device, balance that with the TCO for the pages produced, and make a judgment of whether users are using them at high levels or if the devices are being wasted.

However, There are new color technologies just becoming available that blur the line between a "pure" color printer and a "pure" monochrome printer. The implication is that it won't matter whether the users print only monochrome or both mono and color pages; the relative cost-per-page (all factors considered) will be the same as they would on separate devices.

AVERAGE CPP FOR COLOR PRINTING

See: *Average-Cost-Per-Page* and *% Of Color and Monochrome Devices* above

DEVICE FEATURES AND FUNCTIONS

The question to ask is: Do users have the requisite features and functionality in the available fleet necessary to get their jobs done in the most efficient manner? The way to determine this is to conduct user feedback sessions (or interviews, surveys, etc.) and user-related DISC workflow assessments.

Older devices typically lack many of the new, helpful features available on many new devices today.

PERCENTAGE OF PAGES BY TYPE/SIZE

(Also see: *Percentage of On-glass 11" x 17"/A3* above). Many companies purchase printers and MFPs and don't activate the feature that tracks the number of pages produced on the device by type (on the MFPs). This metric will be useful in helping determine the number of devices and features required to handle user demand. It is a good way to avoid deploying a fleet of devices that are doomed to the status of "waste and excess capacity" as soon as they are installed.

Also, the type of pages-produced-by-percentage will help you in the solution design effort. For instance, if you know the percentage of color, large format, etc. pages produced, you can design your fleet accordingly..

TYPES/QTY OF PAGES PRODUCED ON MFPs

See: *Percentage of Pages by Type/Size* above

One of the biggest office output challenges for companies is deciding how to manage personal printers. Personal printers are one of the major contributors to high cost and waste in the office for reasons described in *STAGE 6: Synthesize The Data and Analyze The Environment* above. But although companies know that controlling personal printers is necessary for a more efficient office output environment, many managers struggle with just how to do it.

I frequently get requests from customer to offer suggestions on how to deal with the growth of personal, non-shared printers in the general office. Over the years, I have worked with many customers that have tried different approaches for managing personal printer growth and reducing their associated costs. Some of these ideas have worked, while many have not. In this section I will share some of the best practices that have actually been effective — to varying degrees — at helping companies control personal printer-growth and the cost of having them in the workplace.

PERSONAL OR NON-SHARED PRINTERS ARE NOT ALL BAD. Before I continue, I'd like to make the point that, in my opinion, personal printers are not all bad and they do have a place in the workplace. I recommend using personal printers primarily as a niche solution. If there is a function that is not being provided in the shared-printer fleet and there are no plans to provide it, then that could be a good use for a personal printer, assuming the person's work "justifies" it (more on that later).

Other things such as a person's physical limitations or one's status in the company could also justify the need for a personal printer. I believe personal printers should be provided based on whether or not their need is justifiable according to some set of criteria determined by the company (I have provided a few best practices below).

WHERE THEY COME FROM/HOW WE GET THEM IN. In my experience, the majority of personal printers — over the last few years at least — have come from end users. In most of these cases, the company sets departmental from end users. In most of these cases, the company sets departmental budgets which allow users in the department to acquire office supplies or other things they need — without IT approval — as long as that item is priced within the budget limit; this budget threshold is often in the range of $1,000 to $1,500. The price of printers is now at such a level that users can get really robust printers for under $1,000. But in interviews with some users, they usually opt for the lowest-priced "nice" printer they see at the local Staples retail store; that device is most often a sub-$200 inkjet printer.

Oftentimes users get fed-up with the print resources available to them in the office so they go out and purchase the inkjet printers out of their own pockets. They sometimes even hide the purchase in an expense account. The point to be made is that users will find a way to get the print resource they need if they feel as though their print requirements are not being met by the current printer fleet available to them.

WHY PERSONAL PRINTERS ARE VILIFIED BY IT MANAGERS. Simply: Cost and support. It is not uncommon for users to acquire personal printers and then have them rolled under the company's support agreement. Plus, when the personal printers have problems, users will place help desk calls and open trouble tickets for the personal printers! This consumes IT resources that could be better spent handling "real" problems. And given the lax printer-consumables purchasing-controls at some companies, it is easy for users to place a call to the purchasing department to order ink cartridges for their personal printers. Users can also go on-line and order the supplies through the company's plan account.

I once performed an engagement with a company that was overrun by personal printers; nearly everybody had one. In addition, the company placed these devices under a support agreement to the tune of $19-per-month plus parts. In effect, they were purchasing a new inkjet printer every year for the employees who had them.

IDEAS FOR IMPROVEMENT. Some of the approaches for dealing with personal printers that I have seen work to varying degrees of success are provided below. It seems as though the stricter the approach, the more effective it is at keeping personal printers under control.

- **MANDATING THE REMOVAL OF PERSONAL PRINTERS AND BANNING THEM.** This approach is at the far-end of the spectrum. Quite simply, the company's CXO will issue a mandate that: "From this day forward no one can own a personal printer, and the personal printers that are in the company today will be removed from your desks. There will be penalties for violating this policy." I worked with a couple of companies that used this approach and, although the most extreme, it was the approach that was most effective at nearly eliminating personal printers.

- **OWNERSHIP BASED ON JUSTIFIABLE "NEED".** Companies using this approach have mandated the removal of all personal printers but have not banned them. Users who could justify the need for a personal printer would get one, and it would be supported centrally by the IT department or the support organization. The personal printers in this case would not typically be small inkjet printers, but instead, they would be low-level networkable printers.

   The justification criteria used by these companies included the items listed below. If the user could answer "yes" to any one of the criteria, the user would be allowed to keep his/her printer (if they have one and if it is an approved printer model) or acquire one through the IT department otherwise.

   THE CRITERIA:

   - Are you a company Executive?
   - Are you an Administrative Assistant to an Executive?
   - Do you have a physical limitation that warrants your own printer?
   - For your job, do you need a feature that is not currently available in your department's shared printer fleet? Explain.
   - Does the performance of your job require that you print more than ____ pages-per-

month?
- – Does your job require that you not leave your desk/office frequently (e.g. call center, physician)?
- – Other

- **KEEP THE PRINTER UNTIL IT DIES.** With this approach, the company will restrict the purchase of new personal printers, and the personal printers that users currently own will not be supported and supplies will not be supplied for them. When the printer dies, the users can not replace it or have it repaired.

- **PROVIDE THE FEATURE THAT PROMPTED THE PURCHASE OF THE PERSONAL PRINTER.** In my years of experience, 95% of users say the reason why they "need" a personal printer is because of something like confidential printing, personal printing, or they support a lot of people. When users state a reason that could be satisfied by a shared printer, the assumption is that if there is a nearby shared printer that offers the features that prompted the personal printer need, the user will be more willing to sacrifice their personal printer. This is the most popular, but least effective approach.

So, what is the right approach for *your* company? Idunno. It depends on your company's level of tolerance for user complaints and your urgency to reduce costs. But acknowledging that your company has a problem in the personal printer fleet — and understand that you may need to take drastic action to address it — is the first step in preparing for what is oftentimes a difficult undertaking. That's why the support of company executives (even the CEO) is highly recommended.

chapter twelve
BUILDING THE BUSINESS CASE

STAGE 8: BUILDING THE BUSNIESS CASE

One bright and sunny Saturday morning, Bob Roberts walked out onto the terrace of his New Jersey beachfront apartment to catch a few rays before heading to the beach for a day of frolicking. While looking down over the herd of hot, thirsty vacationers he was enraptured by an idea that he believed would bring him untold wealth—*a lemonade stand!*

"This," Bob thought, "could be my ticket!" Bob came to this conclusion while observing the masses below. He noticed that there was a constant line of people waiting to be served at the ice cream stand and soda fountain. Surely, he thought, the people would prefer an ice-cold glass of fresh-squeezed lemonade to a sticky, melting ice cream cone.

So Bob sprung into action. He scouted a high-traffic location on the beach where he would set up shop, he created a lemonade recipe that he believed was second-to-none, and he settled on the vision for his lemonade stand business—Bob's Fresh-Squeezed Lemonade:

To become the provider of choice for vacationing families that crave a refreshing glass of fresh-squeezed lemonade.

To put it plainly, Bob wanted to become the "Lemonade King" of the Beach.

That afternoon, Bob began to shop for the ingredients that would produce his sole product —fresh-squeezed lemonade. But Bob didn't just want to create the run-of the-mill glass of lemonade, he wanted to create something special and his ingredients reflected that desire.

THE LEMONS. The lemons for Bob's lemonade would be flown directly from a Florida lemon grove to Bob's apartment via overnight delivery. This way, bob surmised, the lemons would be the freshest possible and would deliver a noticeably fresher taste to his customers.

THE WATER. The water used to constitute Bob's lemonade would be the best! Bob decided that he would drive up to Maine once-a-week and bottle his own water straight from the pure, clean, natural springs from deep in the woods of Maine. This, Bob thought, combined with his fresh lemons, would produce a taste like no other, and customers will be willing to pay a premium for it. Bob would also make his ice from the spring water.

THE SUGAR. Domino? Guess again. Bob decided upon beet sugar as the sweetener for his lemonade. Knowing that sugar beets grow mainly in climates where the soil is rich and the growing season is about five months long, Bob decided to stock-up on the sugar so that he wouldn't be subject to high-prices in the off-sugar beet-season. Once per quarter, he would drive over to a sugar beet farm in Ohio and purchase sugar by the bags full. The sugar, the lemons, and the water—Bob believed—would combine to produce a nectar befitting of the gods.

THE GLASSES. Bob decided to use real crystal glasses instead of paper, plastic, or Styrofoam cups to serve his lemonade. Bob believed the glasses would become souvenirs for the customers so he decided to have his logo printed on the glasses. He also believed that his souvenir glasses would be an added attraction to his lemonade stand.

THE GRAND OPENING

It's opening day for Bob's Fresh-Squeezed Lemonade stand. He set up his booth on the beach, mixed the lemonade, and was ready for business. The logo-emblazoned souvenir glasses were artistically positioned on the counter top, the "Grand Opening" sign flew overhead, the "Buy One Get One FREE!" promotional coupons had been distributed throughout the beach area, and the brand new sign—*"Fresh Lemonade: $10 per-glass!"*—hung at eye-level for all to see.

But after being open for 6-hours, Bob noticed that something unexpected had happened—NOTHING! No customer, no sales, nothing! Bob couldn't understand why no one was buying his pure, refreshing lemonade. Sure, passers-by would approach the stand, but within 10-seconds they would always scrunch-up their faces, shake their heads, snicker, and then walk over to the Coca-Cola stand and buy a soda.

"What is the problem?" he wondered. "Why is no one buying my lemonade?" In an attempt to find an answer to that question Bob checked and double-checked everything. He tasted the lemonade; delicious. He checked-out his stand; clean and inviting. He re-evaluated his location; heavy traffic flow. What is the problem!? Sure, Bob knew that his Lemonade was priced at a premium and was a few dollars-per-glass more expensive than he would have liked, but the cost of his exotic ingredients, souvenir glasses, and travel expenditures had to be recouped and he calculated that this could only be done by charging $10 per glass.

The long day had finally come to a close, and Bob had only made one sale—to an intoxicated young man who thought the price read "$1.00." The young man handed Bob a $10 bill which he thought was a $1 bill. Bob took the money, thanked the young man, and sent him on his merry way complete with a delicious souvenir glassful of lemonade. No harm, no foul.

That night, Bob knew he had to do something to turn his business around. So he decided that he would hire some professionals to help him run the business better.

Before I continue, there are a few things you should know about Bob.

Robert Wentworth Roberts III is a trust -fund baby in the old-money lineage of the *Chicago Roberts*. Robert (or "Bob" as he prefers to be called) never had an appreciation for the value of a dollar. For instance, last month when Bob had a craving for deep-dish pizza, he left his apartment, boarded a plane to Chicago, went to Geno's Original and ordered a deep-dish pizza. He paid for the pizza, returned to the airport and flew right back to New Jersey with the Pizza in-tow.

Bob attended boarding schools as a child and even attended Princeton University for one year before dropping-out to "find himself." Since leaving Princeton, Bob has been living off the reserves in his trust fund. But now Bob has an idea of how he can make his way in the world—Bob's Fresh-Squeezed Lemonade—but the business is not taking-off like he thought it would.

So Bob hired a consultant and some other business professionals to help him turn the business around; he paid each executive $25,000 for the 3-month season. Following the consultant's advice Bob created an organization structure that placed each of the new-hires in charge of one aspect of the operation. Bob created the following positions:

CWO: CHIEF WATER OFFICER. The CWO was responsible for all aspects of water management. His responsibilities included obtaining the pure spring water used in the lemonade recipe; cutting water acquisition costs; planning for the correct amount of water that would be needed for the entire beach season; ice making and maintenance; on-going water management.

CLO: CHIEF LEMON OFFICER. The CLO was responsible for ensuring only the highest-quality of lemon be used in Bob's fresh-squeezed lemonade. Her responsibilities included fresh lemon procurement; reducing the cost of lemon acquisition; making sure that there were enough fresh lemons on-hand at all times to meet demand for the season; on-going lemon management.

CSO: CHIEF SUGAR OFFICER. The CSO was responsible for guaranteeing that no sugar farmer sold them cane sugar in place of Bob's desired beet sugar. She was also responsible for obtaining the beet sugar at the lowest possible price. Her other responsibilities included sugar supply logistics and on-going sugar management.

CPO: CHIEF PRODUCTION OFFICER. The CPO had the dubious task of properly mixing the ingredients in accordance with Bob's lemonade recipe to deliver the standard of lemonade that Bob's Fresh is known for. He was also responsible for quality control and on-going taste approval.

CGO: CHIEF GLASS OFFICER. The CGO was responsible for purchasing the souvenir drinking glasses and having them emblazoned with the company logo. He was responsible for glass inventory, shrinkage management, and reducing the cost of glass acquisition. The CGO was also the company liaison to Bob's outside counsel; so many people complain of cutting themselves on Bob's broken glasses that Bob has had to retain legal counsel.

TMG: THE MARKETING GUY. The Marketing Guy had been hired to help Bob figure out how to sell more lemonade.

Bob charged each of the executives with a straight-forward assignment: put together a plan for how he could sell more lemonade, spend less money, make the customers happier, and turn a profit. The executives went to work with a frenzy—dialing phones, sending e-mails and faxes, taste-testing, negotiating, strategizing, number crunching, hardly bathing, more taste-testing, and so-on, and so-on until their planning was complete!

Signs that your office output Business Strategy might be in need of repair:

1. There is no single department responsible for profit & loss and optimal deployment

2. You don't track office output costs companywide

3. You have not assessed your infrastructure for optimization

4. You are not required to build a business case for major IT projects

5. Your RFP is your business case

6. You don't know what an office output business plan is

THE MEETING

One week later, Bob held a meeting at which the executives would present their plans. The CWO was first up to bat.

THE CWO'S PLAN. The CWO noticed how Bob went about acquiring his spring water and knew there had to be a better way. Heck, the cost of gas, tolls, and lodging alone for Bob's weekly water-bottling trips to Maine cost the company $500 each week.

The CWO wondered if there was really any noticeable difference between the water that Bob bottles himself in Maine, and the Acme-brand spring water that the CWO buys in the local supermarket. He concluded that there was no noticeable taste difference when mixed with lemons and sugar. He also believed that he was supporting Bob's vision of using the finest ingredients since he would still be using spring water instead of tap water or even filtered water.

The CWO then put together a cost comparison between Bob's water acquisition and his Acme-based approach. The results were dramatic and are presented in the table below.

THE CLO'S PLAN. Like the CWO, the CLO noticed that there were some areas of inefficiency in the way Bob procured his lemons. Sure, if we had our druthers we would only use lemons that are plucked straight from the tree. However, unless there's one growing in our yard, most people buy them at farmer's markets or supermarkets.

The CLO also believed that the sweaty, thirsty, hot beachgoers would not know the difference between those lemons that were flown in special and a regular Sunkist lemon found in the supermarket. In fact, she believed, the customer wouldn't even know the difference between Bob's special lemons and frozen lemon concentrate!

So the CLO also developed a cost comparison. [See the Table below]

The CLO's planning showed how she could save Bob nearly $6,000 by using the frozen lemon concentrate, so she decided that would be her recommendation—use the frozen concentrate.

The CSO's Plan. The CSO was a mother of three and visited the beach often with her family. Based on her on experience she didn't think the difference between cane sugar and beet sugar would be noticeable.

When she and her family got thirsty while playing on the beach, they would drink anything that was cold, wet, and half-tasty; they were not too particular about the type of sugar used in their soft drinks, for instance.

So, the CSO decided to recommend using unrefined sugar instead of beet sugar. The taste, she believed, would not be noticeably different and the unrefined sugar fit Bob's strategy of using the finest ingredients. She, too, developed a cost comparison.

THE CGO'S PLAN. As the former social director of his college fraternity, the Chief Glass Officer knew a thing or two about drinking. He also knew which was the cup-of-choice for people who drank in free-n-loose environments like a fraternity—or on a beach. He knew that glass wasn't the answer.

The CGO also knew that the cost of retaining a lawyer—to defend against the many law suits brought by people that cut themselves on Bob's Fresh-Squeezed Lemonade souvenir glasses—was exorbitant.

Putting one-and-one together, he decided that using a plastic translucent cold cup would be the solution. These cups are crystal clear and can even hold custom printing. The biggest advantage, he determined, was that the cups were unbreakable. This would mean no more broken-glass lawsuits. It would also mean a change in his job title to *Chief Container Officer*.

His financial analysis illustrated the financial benefits. [See the Table]

Summary of the Executives' Cost Analysis

Cost Comparison
Ingredient Cost Comparisons for the Season

Cost Category	Water		Lemons		Sugar		Containers		Apple Juice	
	Bob's	CWO's	Bob's	CLO's	Bob's	CSO's	Bob's	CGO's	Bob's	TMG's
Travel & lodging	$8,000									
Plastic bottles	$500	$20								
Bottling permit	$150	$0								
Cost of Water	$0	$790								
Lemon transportation			$2,400	$150					$8,650	$0
Cost of Lemons (Apples / concentrate)			$3,000	$300					$6,400	$800
Lemon Shrinkage			$1,000	$0					$3,800	
Sugar storage space					$500	$350				
Cost of the sugar					$3,000	$20				
Sugar Shrinkage					$300	$0				
Container costs							$8,500	$420		
Glass storage space							$300	$0		
Lawyer's fees							$15,000			
Glass-lawsuit damages							$50,000	$0		
TOTAL COSTS	$8,650	$810	$6,400	$450	$3,800	$370	$73,800	$420	$18,850	$800

145.

The CWO, CSO, CGO, and CLO joined forces and asked the CPO to develop a test batch of the lemonade using the Acme spring water, the unrefined sugar, the Sunkist lemons and the frozen lemon concentrate, then place the finished product in a plastic cups. They wanted to confirm their individual theories that these ingredients would hold up under taste-testing.

When the test batches of lemonade were done, the group of executives worked with The Marketing Guy to do some live customer taste-testing on the beach. The results were generally as expected: the beachgoers could not tell the difference between Bob's lemonade and the Test lemonade. However, the tasters could tell the difference between Bob's lemonade and the frozen lemon concentrate batch of lemonade. They *hated* it!

There was something interesting about the test-tasters' side comments that were overheard by The Marketing Guy. TMG had overheard a few of the beachgoers discuss how much they would enjoy a cold glass of apple juice. Always wanting to break into the ranks of upper-management, TMG had an idea: He could demonstrate his business savvy to Bob by developing a business case for selling cold apple juice! After all, he'd personally overheard some beachgoers express their desire for some apple juice, and he believed he could make the juice a lot cheaper than the cost of Bob's lemonade, especially if he bought Acme-brand apple juice. He developed his financial case as presented in the Table.

During the meeting, each executive presented his/her business plan to Bob. The CWO discussed how Bob could save thousands of dollars and not sacrifice taste or quality by using locally-purchased supermarket spring water. The use of this spring water would also be consistent with Bob's desire to use only the highest-quality ingredients.

The CSO presented her case along the same lines as the CWO: lower cost, no sacrifice in taste, and the use of highest-quality ingredients—in fact, an even higher-quality than Bob's beet sugar. Bob was pleased, but he still had a few questions.

146.

The CLO then presented her frozen lemon concentrate proposal. She describes how Bob could save $6,000 by using the concentrate instead of the imported fresh lemons.

The CGO had an even more compelling story to tell. He illustrated how Bob could reduce his container costs (and other associated costs) by $73,000. Not only was his plastic souvenir cup solution less expensive, but it was also safer and a more user-friendly choice. In addition, the cup did not affect the taste of the juice.

The plastic cup was, admittedly, not as valuable as the souvenir glass, however, one lawsuit by the beach patrol showed that 90% of the glasses Bob sold ended up broken on and around the beach area.

The group of executives then jointly presented how their juice plans would contribute to the attainment of Bob's goals to Increase Sales (same taste, lower selling price, safer container), Reduce Costs (save $87,000 which would allow Bob to sell a cup of lemonade for $2.00), and Improve Customer Satisfaction (better bargain and a safer container resulting in fewer cuts and nasty lawsuits. This would help clean up Bob's image).

The Marketing Guy then proceeded to discuss how Bob could make even more money by selling low-cost apple juice.

After the round of presentations Bob was overall pleased with the work his team had done. But before he asked his first question, he said, "You're fired, and you're fired, and you're fired!" Bob fired three people on the spot.

QUESTION: Whom did Bob fire and why? Think about that before proceeding to the next paragraph.

ANSWER: Bob fired the *Chief Lemon Officer, The Marketing Guy,* and the *Consultant.* He fired the CLO because the CLO presented a solution that was not consistent with Bob's vision. The CLO's recommendation was to use the frozen concentrate which goes against the grain of Bob's vision to sell "Fresh-Squeezed" lemonade. The CLO neglected to propose the Sunkist lemon option which Bob would have accepted.

Bob fired The Marketing Guy for a couple of offenses. The first was for proposing something that was inconsistent with Bob's vision—apple juice. Remember, it's Bob's Fresh-Squeezed *Lemonade*, not Bob's Fresh-Squeezed *Lemonade & Store-Bought Apple Juice!*

And that was the second offense; the apple juice that TMG proposed was not even fresh!

The third offense Bob fired TMG for was for being *clueless!*

The third person Bob fired was the Consultant. Remember: Bob brought these executives in to show him how he could make a profit. The Consultant somehow got amnesia and neglected to tell Bob that he would never make a profit when he factors in the $175,000 cost of the executives' salaries. This Consultant didn't live by my credo: "The discussion might be uncomfortable, but unless you are planning to skip town after the engagement, I suggest you do what's right by the customer."

Alas, Bob's dream of becoming the self-supporting "Lemonade King" was never to be. After realizing he couldn't run a profitable lemonade stand he threw in the towel and shuttered Bob's Fresh-Squeezed Lemonade. Today, Bob is gainfully employed as a salesman for a major computer company.

THE MORAL OF THE STORY

The moral of the story is: Don't drive all the way to Maine to get spring water, and never let The Marketing Guy make business decisions! (I'm just kidding … geez!).

Also, If you happen to be an adult trust-fund baby whose life is going nowhere so you decide to "find your place in the world" by opening a lemonade stand on the beach in an attempt to be crowned the "Lemonade King," do yourself a favor—don't!

The story of Bob's Fresh-Squeezed Lemonade stand is used here to simplistically illustrate how even a seemingly good, money-saving idea can be rejected if it does not support the business objectives of the company or even the objectives of one's superior manager. This has consistently been one of the major challenges facing IT managers as they undertake major technology projects, namely—how to build the business case for a project in order to increase the odds of gaining support and funding for the project from "upper management."

I WANT TO DEVELOP A STRATEGY!

BEFORE I DIG INTO THE DISCUSSION of building the business case I first want to review an area that continues to be a misunderstood topic of confusion, that is—the difference between a *technology strategy* and a *strategic plan* (or business plan) for a technology project.

I often receive requests for assistance from Information Technology (IT) managers that want to develop technology strategies, or more specifically, office output strategies. Many of these managers believe their office output environments (printing, copying, faxing, scanning, document management, processes, etc.) are operating inefficiently without any direction, rhyme or reason. They believe this because individual departments and users purchase equipment out of their own decentralized budgets (often from the local Best Buy technology store), and the result is that nearly everyone has their own printer, fax machine, and/or scanner.

And since there is usually lax adherence to the corporate buying standards, these managers suddenly notice that every technology manufacturer's product is represented throughout the company—there are Hewlett-Packard printers and MFPs, Lexmark printers, Tektronix printers, Canon, Ricoh, and Xerox copiers and MFPs, Epson printers, inkjets, bubblejets, laserjets, deskjets, wax coateds ... you get the idea.

With such overwhelming empirical evidence it is easy to understand why IT managers believe that significant waste exists and their office output environments can and should be operated more efficiently.

One way these managers believe they can achieve such efficiencies and operate the office output environment more effectively is by developing an office output strategy that will guide the activities in the environment. This is where it gets a little confusing.

OFFICE OUTPUT (TECHNOLOGY) STRATEGY

In its simplest terms, an office output (technology) strategy is a plan built around developing, implementing, maintaining, and exploiting a company's office output (technology) assets. It involves identifying technology priorities critical to the company's performance, while matching business needs with that which technology companies has to offer. Or in English: Maximizing the use of office output technology.

An office output strategy could be broadly based to include products, output management, document and content management, workflow processes, management & support, and the like. Any effective technology strategy should be an integral part of a business plan/strategy and, for that reason, I believe that IT organizations should be involved in the business planning process. Firms need business decisions—not technology decisions.

Although a robust office output strategy would—and oftentimes does—include the aforementioned elements (e.g. hardware, document management, etc.), the evidence suggests that as customers look to develop office output strategies they are primarily concerned with getting their arms around the mess that their print, copy, fax, scan, management, support and supplies operations have become. Think about it: In the not-too-distant-past a technology strategy usually consisted of finding the cheapest way to make million-dollar investments in new collections of hardware and software. Even though these kinds of "strategies" have nearly run their course and are no longer viable approaches to meeting business needs, many managers still consider such actions to be a *strategy*, and it is such "strategies" that they have in mind to develop when they ask for assistance.

There are typically two types of conversations that take place which usually go something like this:

CONVERSATION TYPE #1

IT MANAGER: "I want to develop an office output strategy."

ME: "O.k., What are you trying to accomplish?"

IT MANAGER: "I want to put a plan in place that would lead to a more efficient print, copy and fax environment throughout the company."

ME: "Can you elaborate?"

IT MANAGER: "Certainly. I want to put a plan in place that will enable us to procure the right kind of hardware, reduce the number of devices, reduce our costs, and improve user productivity."

At this point in the conversation it starts to become clear that the IT manager doesn't really want to develop a technology strategy as much as a *strategic plan*. The first clue was revealed when the IT Manager began by stating, "I want to put a plan in place..." Subsequent clues were the IT manager's desire to develop a plan to "reduce costs" and "improve user productivity." Such goals are typically the cornerstone of a business plan.

Technology-related business plans will typically involve the creation of IT-initiated projects that inevitably have to be "sold to upper-management" for support and approval. The way these projects and initiatives are best "sold" is through the development of a sound business case (more on this topic later).

(Note: the terms *Strategic Plan* and a *Business Plan* are often used interchangeably. For consistency throughout this document I will use the term *Business Plan*).

CONVERSATION TYPE #2

IT MANAGER: "I want to develop an office output strategy."

ME: "O.k., What are you trying to accomplish?"

IT MANAGER: "I want to develop a strategy for dealing with personal printers and printer vs. MFP deployment issues."

This is more akin to a *technology strategy* whereby the IT Manager wants to maximize the use of office output technology. Simply put, a *strategy* is nothing more than a plan of action and the reality of the matter is that a technology strategy can be something as simple as deciding to refresh office printers every three-years. Something this basic could be considered a printer strategy, or at least a subset of one.

Such discussions with IT managers are often the most difficult related to strategy and business plans because, in many cases, the manager has a hard time coming to grips with the fact that what they are asking for is not the development of a straight-forward technology strategy per-se, but instead the development of a business plan/strategy which involves a far greater level of complexity. It is important to make this distinction before proceeding so that, as we discuss subsequent topics, the reader can put his/her planning interests into the proper perspective.

BUSINESS PLAN

Corporate Strategy, Business Strategy, Strategic Plan, Business Plan ... HUH? What are all of these types of strategies and plans? How are they different? How are they interrelated? When should you use which? I know ... it can get a bit confusing.

Over the years, different management gurus and consultants have modified the basic tenets of business planning in an effort to create planning processes that they could lay claim to. Such self-interest has contributed to the confusion of everything from the definition of an "objective" to the terms we use to describe basic business planning. So I'm going to try to simplify it for you.

A *business plan* is typically designed to establish a framework for management to use as they pursue the organization's objectives. It can also be used to convince an investor that a capital investment in an enterprise's business is a sound financial decision. It defines such things as:

- The company or business unit's goals, objectives, and the strategies used to achieve those objectives.

- The resources required to implement the strategies

- Roles & responsibilities

- The company's business risks

The business plan can be considered the foundation. A *business strategy*, *corporate strategy*, and even a *strategic plan* can be developed in support of an overall business plan. However, many people use the terms interchangeably. So when you get right down to it—the way they're used today—they're all basically the same thing (I know the purists out there are rolling-over in their *Funk and Wagners*).

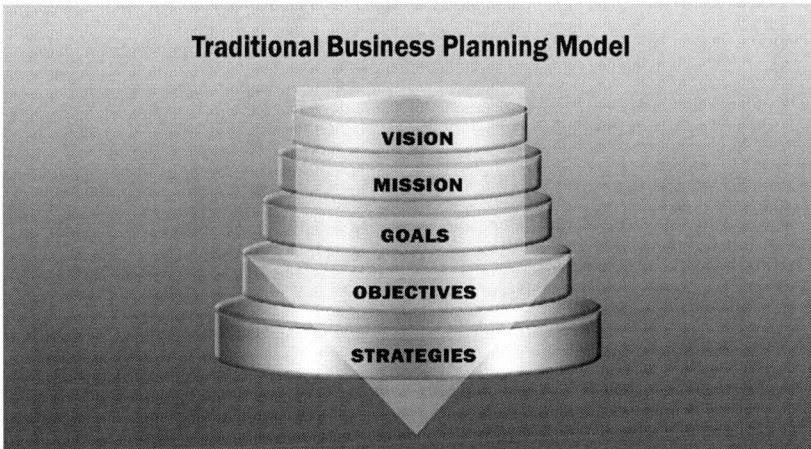

Traditional Business Planning Model

VISION

MISSION

GOALS

OBJECTIVES

STRATEGIES

BUILDING THE BUSINESS CASE

First of all, what is a business case? There are a few different answers to this question depending on your purview. However, this general definition seems to capture the essence of what a business case is:

A business case is a management proposition supporting an investment or procurement judgment. It supports the adoption of a specific solution by a specific organization. The business case is typically prepared for decision-makers in order to obtain project approval to proceed and/or to secure funding for proposed initiatives.

Generally speaking, a business case is a justification process that companies use for project selection. It provides the details of how delivering on the project in question will affect and contribute to the corporate strategy. The business case can further be developed into a *business plan* with the addition of more details.

Many projects get developed in companies but half of them never come to fruition, due in part to the fact that the projects were not developed and supported by a sound business case.

A sound business case is not only the best way to present a project for approval, but it can also reveal whether or not the project is even worth pursuing. Far too often, IT managers undertake technology projects following a hopeful process that I call the "I Like it and So Will Everyone Else" approach. Here's an example:

- The IT manager gets an idea for how to make "improvements"
- The IT manager gets the technology vendor(s) to develop a proposal for a solution that will deliver the envisioned "improvements"
- The IT manager calculates approximately how much today's process costs and implores the vendor(s) to make their proposed solution cheaper.
- The IT manager thinks of some potential non-financial benefits the "improvements" project will provide.
- He combines these potential benefits with the cost savings provided by

the vendors' proposals and presents his project to upper-management for go-forward approval and funding.

- Upper-management is not moved. The project never happens.
- The IT manager begins to wonder, "Why?"

Naturally, there are many possible answers to the question "Why?" In my opinion, if the IT manager revisited the project — this time developing a thorough *business case* for the project —he would likely understand where the project falls down. Conversely, if the IT manager had developed a thorough business case up front, he would have probably begun to see how either his project was sellable or not viable.

Truth be told, developing a thorough business case for a project can be a time-consuming activity because it requires that each aspect of the problem and potential solution be scrutinized and somehow tied back to the objectives of the company, business unit and/or upper management. If this linkage can't be made then the IT manager must honestly determine whether or not the project is worth pursuing. Consider the following simplistic example:

The CIO's objectives for the year are to: *reduce headcount and to eliminate capital spending on technology acquisitions.* The IT manager that reports to the CIO came up with an idea that would save the company significant dollars over the next three years, with the savings beginning to flow in year two. In order to implement the IT manager's project she would need to hire two people and spend $500,000 on new hardware. The IT manager presents her idea to the CIO and the CIO rejects the plan. The IT manager wonders, "Why?"

If the IT manager had developed a thorough business case she would have discovered that the project would not be supported by the CIO because her plan totally contradicted the CIO's objectives.

The CIO and all executive managers are charged with certain responsibilities which they develop business plans to address. Their expectation is that their subordinates' efforts are driven by their objectives and strategies. Any efforts that are not in support of these business plans are—in the opinion of most executive managers—wasted efforts.

DEVELOPING THE BUSINESS CASE

Over the years that I have developed business cases with companies, one thing I found to be consistently true is that executive managers to whom these business cases must be sold expect that a level of diligence and thought has been applied to the project. And many expect that the following business case framework elements have been considered:

- Project Plan/Purpose (Business Plan/strategy)
- Benchmark
- Recommended Future State
- Technology Assessment
- Expected Changes
- Total Cost of Ownership Analysis
- Cost/Benefit Analysis
- Project Timeline
- Risk Assessment
- Results Validation

This is a summarized framework that I use for its simplicity, relevance, and practical completeness. I know of other consultants that use more categories (such as market analysis and sensitivity analysis) or fewer categories (less risk assessment and change analysis). Different decision-makers may require different categories be used, but in general, this outline of categories is rather typical in a business case.

As I explore the business case development process I will use Bob's Fresh-Squeezed Lemonade for illustration purposes where possible. After all, since I made you read that long story the least I can do is make use of it throughout this document.

PROJECT PURPOSE. It could be argued that the project's Purpose is one of—if not the most important aspect of the business case development process. That's because the project Purpose defines the reason for the project's consideration and existence. It answers the question: *Why is this project being developed and what are we ultimately trying to accomplish by investing in it?*

The project's statement of purpose should be clear, meaningful, and agreed-upon because it will ultimately become the guiding principle that drives the activities of the project team. It is extremely important that the project purpose be honestly reviewed and critiqued to ensure that it is in alignment with (and will directly supports) the company's and executives' goals and objectives.

The purpose statement for Bob's Fresh-Squeezed Lemonade could be: *To provide the hot, sticky, sweaty, thirsty beachgoers with a refreshing, all-natural beverage alternative —fresh-squeezed lemonade—made from the finest, freshest ingredients known to man.*

From the project's purpose should flow the specific, measurable goals and objectives of the project. Each goal should be supported by objectives that are measurable and time-specific. In some cases the business unit will have already developed a well-documented business plan. In such cases it is optional whether the project IT Manager chooses to develop a project-specific business plan as part of the project's business case.

The goals for Bob's Fresh-Squeezed Lemonade were:

- To increase lemonade sales
- To reduce the costs of lemonade ingredients
- To improve customer satisfaction with the Bob's Fresh-Squeezed Lemonade brand

Although not specifically stated in this story, an objective to Bob's goal to "reduce costs" could be: To reduce the monthly spend for fresh lemons by 60% over the next two-weeks.

As you develop your business purpose you should ensure that the goals and objectives you develop (that will drive your strategies, needs, and action items) directly support and contribute to the attainment of the company's objectives.

BENCHMARK: *The Current State.* In order to determine whether or not the project will actually provide benefits and improvements, you first must have a benchmark of the way things are today—the Current State.

For instance, if Bob (of Bob's Fresh-Squeezed Lemonade) wanted to reduce the cost of lemonade ingredients, then his executives must know the amount of money Bob is spending today for those ingredients. Likewise, if Bob wants to improve his customers' satisfaction level he must first know the current measure of their dissatisfaction.

In the office output arena companies will oftentimes perform benchmarking studies, gap analyses, and/or environmental assessments as a means of determining such current state variables as total cost-of-ownership (TCO) and overall inefficiency. Once the benchmark is determined and a clear snapshot of today's situation is developed, companies will then be able to use this data as the basis for measuring the proposed benefits to be provided by the project.

RECOMMENDED FUTURE STATE. Using the current state snapshot as a benchmark and the inefficiencies inherent therein, companies can develop solutions that could potentially fix the problems that exist in the current state. Companies should also develop solutions and processes that will contribute to the achievement of the project objectives as determined in the Project Purpose stage.

This is one of the main stages of the process where many business cases fall apart. The reason is often because the IT Manager will have a solution in mind that he/she believes will deliver some set of benefits and/or cost savings to the company. And the manager becomes so convinced that it's the right thing to do, that they become undisciplined and fail to judge that project against the project plan's requirements. This not only could result in a solution that is practically irrelevant, but also the manager's time and energies are wasted since they are not being focused on the achievement of the company's or project plan's objectives.

You have to consider that the development of a business case is in so many ways a business plan or business strategy. And developing a strategy is as much about deciding what not to do as it is what to do.

For example, in the case of Bob's Fresh-Squeezed Lemonade, if Bob had issued a mandate saying, "We will not sell anything other than lemonade," then The Marketing Guy would certainly have known not to waste his time building a case for selling apple juice.

Strategy is about maintaining focus and should define how you channel all of your resources and energy. Any energy expended elsewhere eventually harms your business.

TECHNOLOGY ASSESSMENT. When it comes to office output technology, managers should make sure the technology that's being proposed for the project complies with corporate standards, and that it's appropriate to the needs and requirements of the user community, applications, and workflow processes.

If there are any new technologies being introduced as part of the project plan, these new technologies and their effects should be described and even possibly included in the Expected Changes section.

EXPECTED CHANGES. Major office output projects inevitably require some kind of change. Whether it's a physical environmental change, user process change, technology change or application change, the expected changes will usually require some form of change management planning. The effects of the change could also lead to a modification in the project plan and business case.

Changes that are expected to result from the project's implementation can also have an effect on level of risk the company will have to assume and they can affect modifications to the physical infrastructure. Such changes could have an effect on the project's financial projections and they can even lead to a "no-go" decision if the anticipated effects are dramatic enough.

Organizational changes that are expected to occur during the life of the project should also be accounted for in the project plan. If the company is planning to down-size over the next 12-months, for example, then such changes should be scoped into the plan. Even future technology introductions by hardware manufacturers can result in a modification to the project plan.

In the case of Bob's Fresh-Squeezed Lemonade, the Chief Glass Officer proposed the use of plastic cups instead of crystal drinking glasses. If this plan was implemented, then Bob would eliminate the broken-glass lawsuits and help clean up his image.

TOTAL COST OF OWNERSHIP (TCO) ANALYSIS. In the office output environment, Total Cost of Ownership is defined as the total cost of owning an asset and making that asset available to users over an extended period of time. By now, most managers know that their total cost of ownership for printing, copying, faxing, and digitizing goes beyond just the cost of the device and the supplies & consumables for the device. When calculating TCO most companies will use some combination of the Hardware, Maintenance/ Support Costs, Software, Consumables, Network Management/Administration costs, Infrastructure costs, and End-user Operations/ Lack of Availability costs.

Determining TCO is crucial to understand the true cost of having a project's solution implemented. Not understanding and appropriately determining the TCO could result in an inaccurate assessment of a project's costs and potential savings.

At Bob's Fresh-Squeezed Lemonade, the Chief Glass Officer calculated Bob's TCO for using souvenir crystal drinking glasses. The CGO not only included the obvious cost of the glasses alone, but also included the other costs that were associated with Bob's use of crystal drinking glasses, including the cost for a lawyer, broken drinking-glass lawsuits, and the cost of storing palates of drinking glasses. The inclusion of these costs is legitimate because Bob would not incur these costs if he did not use crystal drinking glasses.

If the CGO did not take these costs into consideration, then the savings projections from his proposed use of plastic cups would have been inaccurate and not as significant; this could have resulted in Bob rejecting his proposal outright.

COST/BENEFIT ANALYSIS. Many companies use cost/benefit analyses to determine the impact and worthiness of a project. Some companies even go so far as to mandate that all projects have a Return-on-Investment (ROI) that exceeds some threshold and that the project pays for itself within a certain time period.

The first steps in developing a cost/benefit analysis should be determining all of the project's associated costs and potential benefits, and assigning a dollar-value to the benefits. Once you have defined these costs & benefits, and have gathered other relevant data, you can begin to make calculations.

There are several metrics—some useful, some not so useful—that are used in a cost/benefit analysis for decision-making purposes, including:

Present Value (PV). Present Value is simply the value of a cash flow stated in today's dollars. It is the value of an ongoing benefits discounted back to the present year. The formula for calculating present value is as follows:

$$PV = \left[\frac{\text{Net Cash Flow Year 1}}{(1 + \text{Discount Rate})}\right] + \left[\frac{\text{Net Cash Flow Year 2}}{(1 + \text{Discount Rate})^2}\right] + \left[\frac{\text{Net Cash Flow Year N}}{(1 + \text{Discount Rate})^N}\right]$$

The formula for calculating Present Value also serves as the foundation for calculating other cost/benefit metrics, including Net Present Value, Return on Investment, and Internal Rate of Return.

Net Present Value (NPV). NPV is the value of the ongoing benefits discounted back to the present year, net of the initial capital outlay. This metric tells you if the project should *not* be undertaken, but it doesn't tell you to proceed. A general rule-of-thumb is that if the NPV calculation is less than zero, you should scrap the project. the formula for NPV = (PV - initial capital outlay)

Return on Investment (ROI). ROI is probably the most important metric to use for choosing and prioritizing projects within a company. ROI allows you to compare the attractiveness of one investment over another. While ROI tells you what percentage return you will see on your investment over a specified period of time, it does not tell you about the magnitude of the project. In other words, a project with a ROI of 200% sounds better than a project with a ROI of 10%. But if the returns are 200% of $10,000 versus 10% of $20M, then the 200% return doesn't seem so attractive (relatively) after all.

The formula for ROI = (PV/initial capital outlay)

Break-even Point (Payback Period). This is the time it takes for benefits returned to equal the initial cost of the project. In the office output technology area where technologies are constantly evolving and improving, this could serve as measurement of risk. Some companies are looking for payback periods of less than one year on certain types of projects! But I wouldn't recommend using this metric as the single determining factor for making go, no-go decisions on projects.

The formula for calculating Payback Period = (initial investment/ average cash flow)

Internal Rate of Return (IRR). IRR equals the percentage rate by which you have to discount the cashflows (net benefits) until the point that they equal the initial costs.
In other words, the Internal Rate of Return is the discount rate that makes the project have a zero Net Present Value.

Companies will usually only approve projects or investment where the

IRR is higher than the cost of capital, or in other words, where the NPV will be greater than zero.

This calculation is not straight-forward. It is the NPV where the discount rate = zero. Whenever I have to calculate IRR, I use a spreadsheet, calculate NPV, and continually adjust the discount rate until I come up with a NPV of zero; believe it or not, this is probably the easiest way to do it.

For example, if there's a project with the following characteristics:

- Initial investment = $10,000
- Net cash flow = $5,000/year for 3 years
- Discount Rate (cost of capital) = 10%

In this example, the Present Value = $12, 434 (see the calculation below)

$$\$12,434 = \left[\frac{\$5,000}{(1+.10)}\right] + \left[\frac{\$5,000}{(1+.10)^2}\right] + \left[\frac{\$5,000}{(1+.10)^3}\right]$$

The NPV = $2,434; the ROI = 124%; the IRR = 23%; and the Break-even = 2 years.

Cost/benefit analysis can be very complex or something simple and straight-forward such as: "How much money will we make and how much will it cost us to make that amount of money?" If the consultant at Bob's Fresh-Squeezed Lemonade, decided to do a cost/benefit analysis for the lemonade stand project, he would have discovered the NPV was less than zero due to Bob's high salary costs, and would have advised Bob to scrap the idea in its current iteration.

Different companies have different criteria and require certain metrics be calculated beyond the ones mentioned here. For instance, companies may use simple TCO as their cost/benefit analysis requirement. There's just no single way to slice it.

PROJECT TIMELINE. A traditional project schedule should be developed that illustrates major milestones, dependencies, and the key stages of the project's implementation ranging from analysis, to testing, to review and analysis.

RISK ASSESSMENT. A risk assessment should be developed as a process to identify potential risks, determine resolution actions, and track the project team's progress in reducing risks that could impede the team's progress in achieving the project objectives.

Companies follow structured risk management routines that include several activities including (but not limited to): Identifying the risks, assessing the risks, planning the response to the risk, monitoring the risks on an on-going basis, and developing a risk contingency plan.

In the case of Bob's Fresh-Squeezed Lemonade, the executives identified a potential risk by changing Bob's lemonade ingredients list to include Acme spring water, unrefined sugar, and Sunkist lemons in plastic cups. Their response to this risk was to do taste-testing with the beachgoers. They could monitor the beachgoers' satisfaction with the potion daily, and their contingency plan could be to revert to Bob's old ingredients but find a cheaper way to procure them.

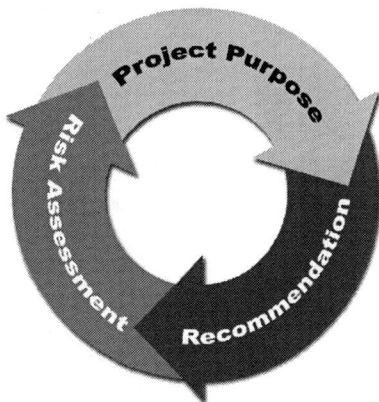

RESULTS VALIDATION. "How do we determine whether or not the projected benefits of the solution are actually being (or have been) achieved? How do we prove that the project is delivering on the promise it was sold on?" How often do we hear that question? This is a question that executives are asking of IT managers as the managers propose major office output projects.

One reason for this line of questioning is because, over the years, projects have been sold by IT Managers to executives that yield marginal benefits at best, and negative results at worst.

The simplest way companies attempt to validate the expected results of a project is by setting up pilots of the solution and testing the logic of the plan in a real-world setting.

In an effort to assign accountability for the delivery of the expected benefits of office output projects, managers are working with boutique consulting firms and office output manufacturers on ways to measure and validate the results of the projects that have been and are being implemented. This feedback can be used to determine the "success" of a project.

The feedback is also commonly being used by managers to determine where modifications are required in the solution and/or the project plan if the project is not delivering the expected benefits. And since the project plan is a living document it should be updated and modified as new information dictates, and as results that fall below expectations warrant.

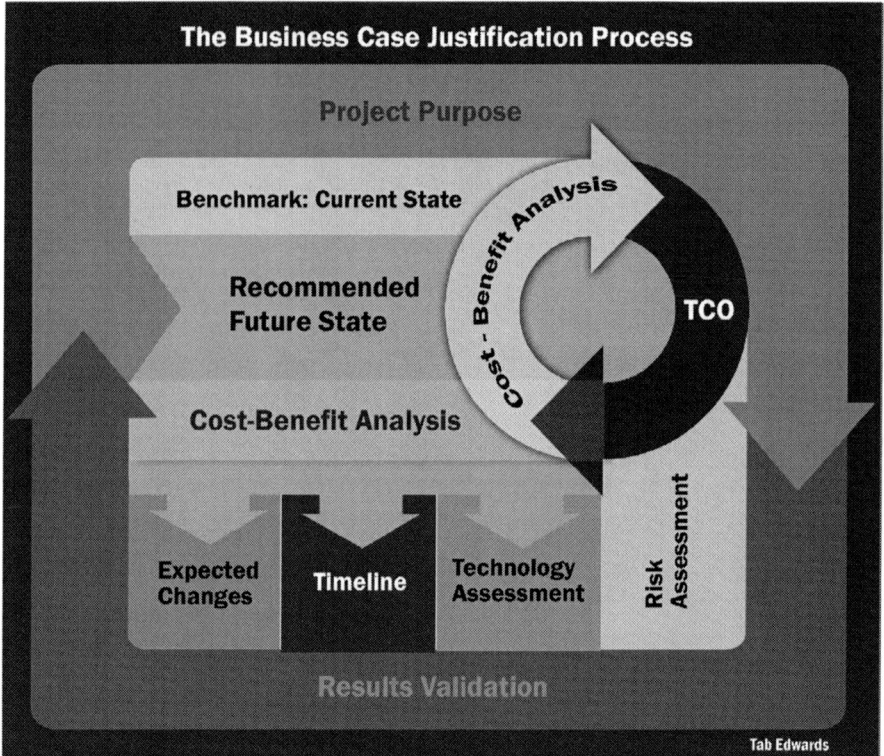

The Business Case Justification Process

Project Purpose

Benchmark: Current State

Cost - Benefit Analysis

Recommended Future State

TCO

Cost-Benefit Analysis

Expected Changes

Timeline

Technology Assessment

Risk Assessment

Results Validation

Tab Edwards

CONCLUSION

Building a business case is simply a tool that forces you to consider all aspects and likely outcomes of a planned project. Obviously, lots of projects get approved and funded without having to submit to the rigors of a business case. And lots of companies simply need to see that a company will reduce costs or make money in order to fund it.

But in most cases, the numbers are not enough to get project approval. And when you think about it, if diligence has not been applied to the calculations, the numbers don't always add up. Consider the following:

"Any time Detroit scores more than 100-points and holds the other team below 100-points, they almost always win."
(Doug Collins, TV pro basketball analyst)

"That was Andy Benes' fifth strikeout on the day. He came in with 94, so now he has 104 strikeouts on the year."
(Ralph Kiner)

"I'm gonna give you 110% on every play. You can't give any more than that."
(Jimmy Johnson, U. of Illinois quarterback)

"This fight is going to be 90% mental and 50% physical"
(Lou Duva, boxing manager)

The point I'm trying to make is that decisions are made and supported for lots of different reasons — some financial and some not. In order to maximize the probability of gaining acceptance of your office output project proposal, the level of diligence that is forced by the creation of a thoughtful business case — *eleven times out of ten* — can be your best ally.

chapter thirteen

FRAGMENTED OWNERSHIP & THE BENEFITS OF CENTRALIZATION

Illustration: Joshua Black, Blackeyesoup.com

FRAGMENTED PURCHASE AND PROFIT & LOSS RESPONSIBILITY, AND THE BENEFITS OF CENTRALIZATION (CONVERGENCE)

BACKGROUND

In most corporations the hardcopy infrastructure (the printers, copiers, fax machines and scanners) has, until recent years, been an area of the organization that has not received a lot of focus. This is truer for the printer infrastructure than for the copier infrastructure. There are several reasons that Chief Information Officers offer to explain this condition, the most common being that the printers are inexpensive and they work, so in the grand scheme of things it's just not that critical an area to focus on.

This had been the prevailing attitude until Information technology (I/T) managers were forced to look outside of the data center for other areas to generate cost savings. As manager began conducting assessments of their Document-Related Information Supply Chain (DISC) and hardcopy infrastructures, they consistently found the following conditions to be true:

- The waste and high-costs were worse than they had imagined
- Overall device and cost information were unknown to them
- There was a high concentration of devices per user, leading to excess capacity
- The devices were old and inefficient
- Devices were purchased without regard for a deployment strategy
- Similar devices and supplies were being purchased separately by I/T, Facilities & Operations (including Purchasing), and end-user departments
- There was an opportunity to significantly reduce costs and save money

As companies began developing strategies to improve their hardcopy environments, one thing became clear: it will be very difficult implement an efficient, cost-saving solution and sustain the savings without a change in the organizational policies & procedures around requesting, purchasing, paying for, maintaining responsibility for, and owning hardcopy assets.

UNDERSTANDING THE PROBLEM

Since the mid-'90s - when spending on hardware was unprecedented - companies have become overwhelmed by the number of printers, copiers and fax machines that proliferate throughout their offices leading to high costs and excess capacity. Today, we find that the primary causes for general high costs and inefficiency are a result of the following conditions: Failure to Manage, Fragmented Responsibility and not taking advantage of Improvements in Technology. This paper will focus on Fragmented Responsibility.

In most corporations multiple departments have authority and profit & loss responsibility that overlap in the office hardcopy environment. For instance, the I/T, Facilities & Operations, and User Departments may each have the ability to purchase printers, MFPs and supplies, while doing so under no overall deployment strategy. As a result, companies will have a high percentage of personal-use printers, "too many" devices of a similar type, and multiple models of the same technology. The result is not only a duplication of effort, but duplication of costs, waste and excess capacity driven by:

- Fragmented purchase and profit & loss responsibility
- The lack of a single department responsible for optimal deployment

A discussion about organizational fragmentation cannot begin until a company's process for acquiring, paying for, supporting, and ultimately owning hardcopy technology is reviewed. The process a company typically follows can reveal a great deal about the degree of fragmentation that exists and the areas of inefficiency (concern) inherent in the process.

ACQUISITION, SUPPORT and OWNERSHIP PROCESS. The typical acquisition, support and ownership model (for hardcopy technology) that is followed by most companies generally flows as illustrated in the diagram below:

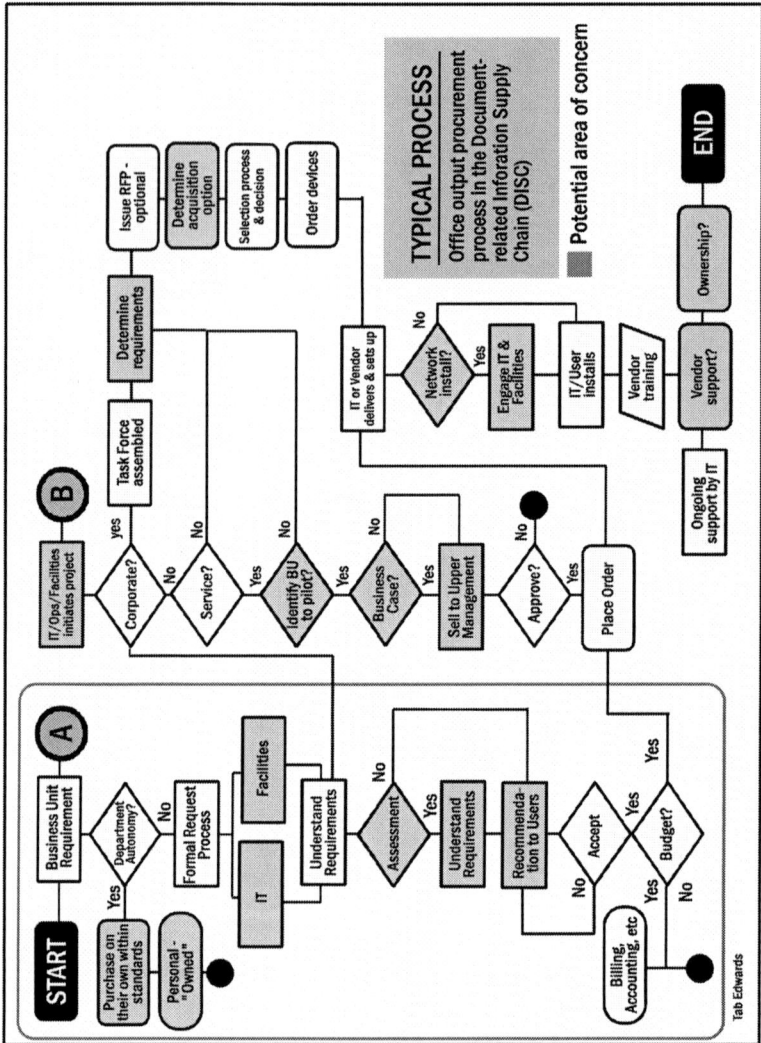

TYPICAL PROCESS

Office output procurement process in the Document-related Inforation Supply Chain (DISC)

■ Potential area of concern

START → Business Unit Requirement → Department Autonomy?

Yes → Purchase on their own within standards → Personal - "Owned"

No → Formal Request Process → IT / Facilities → Understand Requirements → Assessment

Assessment: No / Yes → Understand Requirements → Recommendation to Users → Accept

Accept: No / Yes → Budget? → No → Billing, Accounting, etc → Yes

A

IT/Ops/Facilities initiates project → B

B → Task Force assembled → Corporate?

Corporate? yes / No

Service? No / Yes → Identify BU to pilot? No / Yes → Business Case? No / Yes → Sell to Upper Management → Approve? No / Yes → Place Order

Determine requirements → Issue RFP - optional → Determine acquisition option → Selection process & decision → Order devices

IT or Vendor delivers & sets up → Network install? No / Yes → Engage IT & Facilities → IT/User installs → Vendor training → Vendor support? → Ownership? → END

Ongoing support by IT

Tab Edwards

Scenario "A" represents to the case whereby the user department initiates a request for hardcopy technology. Scenario "B" represents the case whereby the I/T and/or Facilities/Ops/Purchasing department(s) initiate a project for the procurement of hardcopy technology. The yellow highlighted boxes represent areas of concern or potential inefficiency in the process.

"SO WHAT?"

The process by which corporations determine requirements for, orders, and assigns "ownership" to hardcopy devices (the diagram above) could lead to increased costs and inefficiency throughout the organization where such a model is applicable. The potential areas of concern include:

- **FRAGMENTATION: AN INCREASE IN THE NUMBER OF PERSONAL PRINTERS.** When users have the autonomy and budget to acquire printers (even if it is done within the constraints of a standards list), the result is a high percentage of personal printers. A survey of personal printer users across multiple corporations revealed that 90% of these users said that the reason they used a personal printer is because they print confidential or secure documents in the course of their daily work activities.

In most cases, the user departments have a limited capital budget (typically $1,000) which can be used to purchase office technology (code name: "office supplies"). When a user doesn't believe that his/her print requirements are being met by the shared printers in the department, then the user will inevitably use their office supplies budget to buy a printer either through the company's on-line requisition system or by simply going down to the local office supplies store (e.g. Staples) and expensing it. As a result, most companies are inundated with personal printers. This behavior will continue as long as user departments have the autonomy to purchase printers ("office supplies") and the budget (local Profit & Loss responsibility) to do so. If the average annual Total Cost of Ownership (TCO) of a supported personal printer is $250, and the personal printer-to-user ratio (in a 10,000 person corporation), is 1-to-4, then the cost of waste and ex-

EXAMPLE: THE PROBLEM WITH FRAGMENTATION

A typical 10,000 person company and how they address their requirements for hardcopy technology.

COST ASSUMPTIONS: Uses all TCO cost elements in determining costs: annual TCO cost for a personal printer is $250; MFP is $5,500; shared printer is $3,500.

	THE SITUATION	THE WASTE (All Users)
USER DEPARTMENT WITH 20 USERS 	The users at the department level have the budget and the autonomy to purchase printers. Many users believe they "need" a printer for confidentiality, and they will use their budget to order them. In this scenario, user departments purchase 5 printers - including department-class printers.	TCO Cost: $625,000 Excess: $500,000
FACILITIES & OPERATIONS/PURCHASING 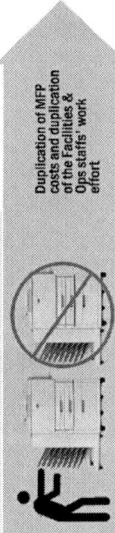 Duplication of MFP costs and duplication of the Facilities & Ops staffs' work effort	The Facilities & Ops department is faced with the lease expiration of their existing copier fleet. They upgrade the fleet to newer devices (MFPs), and for simplicity, they maintain the same quantity of devices - they do not reduce the fleet size. They own the P&L for these devices, even though they charge-back the user departments for usage.	TCO Cost: $8,250,000 Excess: $2,772,000
INFORMATION TECHNOLOGY DEPARTMENT  Duplication of MFP costs, printer costs and duplication of the I/T staffs' work effort	The I/T department notices that the printer fleet is old and some printers are failing. They order new network (shared) printers as well as some MFPs to help improve user productivity. They order the MFPs without the benefit of an integrated plan with Facilities & Ops. The I/T department maintains te P&L for their hardcopy devices.	TCO Cost: $3,500,000 Excess: $1,750,000
	TOTAL EXCESS SPEND	$5,022,000 (40%)

⊘ In an integrated, less fragmented environment these devices would not be needed cess capacity in personal printers could be more than $500,000 annually. [See the diagram]

- **FRAGMENTATION: INTERNAL CONFLICT BETWEEN I/T AND FACILITIES/OPERATIONS.** As corporations introduce office-class multifunction devices/peripherals (MFPs), the potential for conflict and duplication of effort related to the acquisition and "ownership" of the devices exists. Typically, both organizations can determine the standards for, purchase, support and own responsibility and budget for MFPs. This duplication of effort is not productive and it could lead to multiple MFP models and manufacturers throughout the organization.

One major problem of fragmentation related to the acquisition if MFPs is that, although both I/T and facilities/Ops can purchase MFPs (since they have the autonomy and P&L responsibility), the two departments often make purchase decisions independent of each other and the user departments. The result is excess capacity due to the duplication of MFPs (and the fact that more often than not, the MFPs are acquired in the absence of a deployment strategy or departmental assessment).

If the average annual Total Cost of Ownership (TCO) of a department-class MFP is $5,500 and the MFP-to-user ratio (in a 10,000 person corporation), is 1-to-3.4, then the cost of waste and excess capacity in MFPs could be more than $2.8Million annually.

- **INAPPROPRIATE MIX OF DEVICES.** In most companies, printer purchases are made without the benefit of an assessment or other method of understanding the users' requirements for output. The result is that printers are being purchased without an overriding plan or deployment strategy. This leads to the purchase and placement of printers that may not be "necessary" to satisfy user requirements for output production, and contributes to excess print capacity, waste, and higher costs.

Contributing to the inefficiency is the fact that both the user departments and the I/T department purchase printers without any significant joint planning or requirements definition. This leads to additional waste and

175.

high costs. For instance, if the average annual Total Cost of Ownership (TCO) of a supported networked (shared) printer is $3,500 and the shared-printer-to-user ratio (in a 10,000 person corporation), is 1-to-10, then the cost of waste and excess capacity in networked/shared printers could be more than $1.8Million annually.

FRAGMENTED PURCHASE AND PROFIT & LOSS RESPONSIBILITIES. As stated previously, in most corporations multiple departments have purchase authority and profit & loss responsibility that overlap in the office hardcopy environment. The I/T, Facilities & Operations, and User Departments may each have the authority to purchase hardcopy products, and they also own the profit & loss responsibility for such acquisitions as illustrated in Diagrams C and D below. This situation exists at most corporations. Fragmented hardcopy responsibility can have negative results including:

- Independent purchase decisions resulting in fleet imbalance and high costs
- Multi-source budgets leading to duplication of spend and higher costs
- Multi-source P&L responsibility for hardcopy resulting in ignored overall corporate costs
- No single department can ensure optimal deployment of technology or strategies
- Uneven buy-in to corporate initiatives such as hardcopy utility models. My experience has shown that when companies attempt to implement corporate-wide balanced hardcopy models (such as managed print solutions) in a fragmented environment where users purchase and "own" their printer and MFP assets, there is often resistance to change. One reason is because only certain costs are visible to users; they might only pay for the printer hardware and supplies out of heir budgets. All other cots are borne by the I/T department. When companies move to a managed print model and institute a charge-back system whereby user departments will now pay for other costs such as support, helpdesk, and some I/T charges,

they oftentimes execute their power to opt-out and not participate in the program. If enough departments follow this course of action throughout the corporation, then the company will not be able to realize he full potential of their balanced/managed print solution strategy.

- The inability to effectively roll-out corporate-wide initiatives

The results of industry engagements show that fragmentation in purchasing, ownership and P&L has resulted in up to 40% of additional cost due to excess equipment being purchased, multiple models of the same equipment being proliferated, loss discounts due to fragmented purchases, and waste due to obsolescence and purchases being made without a shared vision or deployment strategy. The result is that the average 10,000-person company could be wasting as much as $5,000,000 annually due to the fragmented nature of hardcopy responsibility and Profit & Loss.

FRAGMENTED RESPONSIBILITY
DRIVING ENTERPRISE COSTS IN IMAGING AND OUTPUT

Legend:
- Areas of duplicate cost, duplicate P&L responsibility, and/or duplicate effort = lack of clear ownership
- Areas of clear delineation

Rows: LOST DOCUMENTS, SUPPLIES STORAGE, FAX, OUTSOURCED COPY, CRD/MAILROOM, RECORDS MGMT, HELPDESK, SUPPLIES, HARDWARE — each with PROFIT & LOSS and RESPONSIBILITY

Columns: DEPARTMENT, FACILITIES & OPERATIONS, INFORMATION TECHNOLOGY, DEPARTMENT MANAGEMENT, TELECOMMUNICATIONS, FINANCE

CHALLENGES
- Independent decisions > imbalance > higher costs
- Multi-source budgets > duplication > higher costs
- Multi-source budgets > overall costs ignored
- No single department can ensure optimal deployment
- Departmental "control" > uneven buy-in to solutions
- Inability to effectively roll-out corporate-wide initiatives

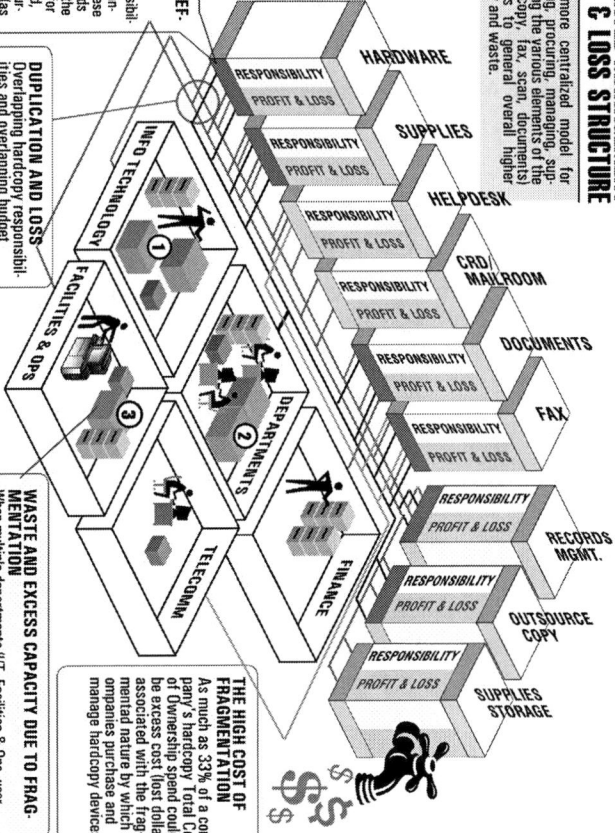

THE FRAGMENTED MANAGEMENT AND PROFIT & LOSS STRUCTURE

The lack of a more centralized model for budgeting, ordering, procuring, managing, supporting, and owning the various elements of the hardcopy (print, copy, fax, scan, documents) environment leads to general overall higher costs, inefficiency and waste.

HIGH COST AND INEFFICIENCY DUE TO FRAGMENTATION

The fragmented Responsibility and Profit & Loss management structure of these various silos directly leads to inefficiency because the overall corporate costs for each element are ignored, there is duplication of purchases and work effort (as illustrated by the RED highlights), and no department is responsible for ensuring that devices are being optimally purchased and deployed.

DUPLICATION AND LOSS

Overlapping hardcopy responsibilities and overlapping budget control for these cost elements leads to inefficiency, confusion, lost dollars, and the inability to effectively implement a balanced deployment model.

WASTE AND EXCESS CAPACITY DUE TO FRAGMENTATION

When multiple departments (I/T, Facilities & Ops, user Departments) have purchase and P&L responsibilities, there will inevitable be a superfluous number of hardcopy devices throughout the company (as illustrated by devices 1, 2 and 3). This results in excess output capacity and waste in the hardcopy fleet of devices.

THE HIGH COST OF FRAGMENTATION

As much as 33% of a company's hardcopy Total Cost of Ownership spend could be excess cost (lost dollars) associated with the fragmented nature by which companies purchase and manage hardcopy devices.

HARDWARE
SUPPLIES
HELPDESK
CRD/MAILROOM
DOCUMENTS
FAX
RECORDS MGMT.
OUTSOURCE COPY
SUPPLIES STORAGE

RESPONSIBILITY
PROFIT & LOSS

INFO TECHNOLOGY
FACILITIES & OPS
DEPARTMENTS
TELECOMM
FINANCE

TOWARDS CENTRALIZATION:
MOVING TOWARDS A LESS FRAGMENTED MANAGEMENT STRUCTURE

As discussed earlier in this document, there are inherent inefficiencies built into the fragmented profit & loss and responsibility model. While moving towards a more centralized approach will yield significant benefits, getting there will require changes in both job responsibilities and P&L ownership. Following are some things to consider along this pursuit.

• Organizational behavioral changes are as, or more, important to success than IT infrastructure changes. Though infrastructure changes will result in the fastest return, organizational changes must be installed and enforced for any sustenance of the cost savings.

• Engage Senior Management. In order for policies to be enforced and to facilitate "buy-in" to the corporate improvement project, senior management must be actively engaged to ensure compliance with any far-reaching changes.

• Choose the scope: department, division, enterprise, internal, external. A decision must be made on how to proceed with the roll-out of the new hardcopy responsibility structure. Is the organization prepared to begin a corporate-wide rollout of the new strategy, or would it be more effective to start with a subset of the organization, gain some learning and experience, and then deploy more broadly?

• Develop new and/or changed roles & responsibilities. Effective institution of a centralized approach to a balanced office deployment model requires that the different departments that are responsible for some aspect of the DISC (e.g. I/T, Facilities & Ops, Department Management, Finance, Telecommunications) coordinate their efforts. Their efforts should be guided by a strategic plan and "team" concepts. The team will have to agree on ownership roles for each hardcopy area referenced in Diagram C above (hardware, supplies, helpdesk, document management, CRD/mailroom, outsourced copy, fax, supplies storage and lost documents). A decision regarding P&L oversight and/or ownership responsibility will have to be agreed upon and enforced. For instance, do you remove the authority to purchase printers from the user departments? If so, will that responsibility fall to the I/T organization?

- Define the team's common line-of-command and dispute Ombudsman. The newly-formed "team" will have to determine the line of command for dispute resolution and ultimate decision-making authority. A recent trend for companies is to create a new position with the title of Output Convergence Officer, Chief Output Manager, "Output Czar," etc. This manager is responsibility for all things DISC and to ensure that output-related initiatives are carried out with a vision for the entire organization. This manager may not "own" P&L for the different areas, but his/her role would be more of an oversight or watchdog capacity to ensure that the corporation's many entities are acting in a coordinated manner as it relates to the document-related information supply chain.

- Develop new policies & procedures. This includes a centralized bill-back solution across the scope of the project (whether it is copiers, MFPs, printers, fax machines or their associated services). New acquisition procedures will have to be developed, and new guidelines (e.g. personal printer guidelines) will have to be instituted and enforced.

- Anticipate and proactively address user resistance to change. It is important to involve user departments in the early stages of this effort. It will be easier to gain their acceptance down the line.

- Pilot the new structure. A decision must be made as to the scope of the roll-out. By departmental? Business unit? By geography? Corporate-wide? Other?

- Adjust based on learning

- Implement

A Document-related Information Supply Chain (DISC) workshop is recommended for companies that are interested in the topic of fragmentation, are considering a move towards centralization (less fragmentation), want to explore the topic in greater detail as it relates to their specific organization's hardcopy model, and/or want to begin the development of a centralization strategy. Please contact your representative for additional information.

THE POTENTIAL BENEFITS

In addition to the work-related benefits that a reduction in duplication of effort will provide, the cost savings that are associated with a move to a less fragmented environment (combined with a hardcopy deployment and management strategy as illustrated in the diagram below) can be as much as 40% or greater. For a typical 10,000 person company this could mean a savings of $5Million annually; $25,000,000 annually for a 50,000 person company.

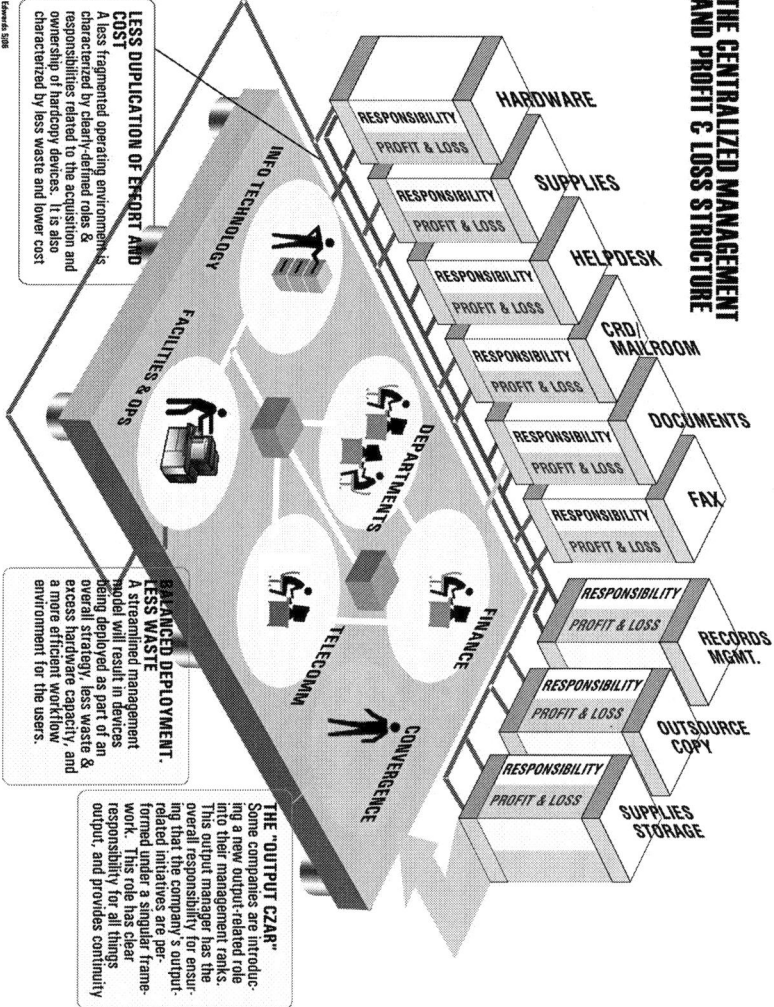

THE CENTRALIZED MANAGEMENT AND PROFIT & LOSS STRUCTURE

Edwards 5/06

LESS DUPLICATION OF EFFORT AND COST
A less fragmented operating environment is characterized by clearly-defined roles & responsibilities related to the acquisition and ownership of hardcopy devices. It is also characterized by less waste and lower cost

INFO TECHNOLOGY

FACILITIES & OPS

DEPARTMENTS

TELECOMM

FINANCE

CONVERGENCE

BALANCED DEPLOYMENT.
LESS WASTE
A streamlined management model will result in devices being deployed as part of an overall strategy, less waste & excess hardware capacity, and a more efficient workflow environment for the users.

THE "OUTPUT CZAR"
Some companies are introducing a new output-related role into their management ranks. This output manager has the overall responsibility for ensuring that the company's output-related initiatives are performed under a singular framework. This role has clear responsibility for all things output, and provides continuity

HARDWARE
RESPONSIBILITY
PROFIT & LOSS

SUPPLIES
RESPONSIBILITY
PROFIT & LOSS

HELPDESK
RESPONSIBILITY
PROFIT & LOSS

CRD/ MAILROOM
RESPONSIBILITY
PROFIT & LOSS

DOCUMENTS
RESPONSIBILITY
PROFIT & LOSS

FAX
RESPONSIBILITY
PROFIT & LOSS

RECORDS MGMT.
RESPONSIBILITY
PROFIT & LOSS

OUTSOURCE COPY
RESPONSIBILITY
PROFIT & LOSS

SUPPLIES STORAGE
RESPONSIBILITY
PROFIT & LOSS

183.

chapter fourteen
TAB'S FEARLESS PROGNOSTICATIONS

AHH ... WHAT THE HELL

Oftentimes when I'm speaking with companies or speaking at seminars I am asked for my opinion on where the (hardcopy) industry is going and what companies can expect in the short, medium and long-terms. And while writing this book, I found myself forming random thoughts about what I believe the whole distributed office output sector and the associated technologies would look like in ten years. Why *ten* years and not, say, 7.36 years? I don't know. Maybe because we like thinking in round numbers. Besides, ten years is a long time from now, and if my predictions are proven to be ridiculously off-track, then no one would remember this book by then, and my reputation will be safe!

So, without further ado ... (hey ... why do we always use the phrase "without further *ado*" before beginning an event? That doesn't really make sense if you think about it. "Ado" means something like hectic activity going on, a lot of commotion. Think about the times you hear people or events being introduced by the emcee saying, "Without further ado ..." That doesn't seem to be an appropriate introduction, does it? Oh, I'm sorry, where was I?).

Oh, I was saying: So, without further *delay*, I now give you my Fearless Prognostications of the future of print, copy, fax and scan in the general office.

[Please note: the views presented here are the opinions and forecasts of Tab Edwards, only, and should not be considered the opinions of any company, business entity or organization. The information provided herein is not the result of any business plans or information (i.e. insider information), undisclosed or otherwise.]

1. EVERY NEW PC WILL COME PRE-CONFIGURED WITH AN INTEGRATED LASER PRINTER/SCANNER

In the next 5 to 7 years, many new personal computers will ship as single units with an attached (integrated) laser printer (think: iMac twice as thick) . The printer portion will be about the size of a laptop computer, it will hold about 25 sheets of paper (fed manually through a slot), and it will be extremely reliable. To top it off, the entire unit (PC with integrated printer) will retail for about $600 after the honeymoon period.

Some of you may be thinking: "That'll never happen. What if the printer portion breaks? It will damage the whole machine and you won't be able to use the PC until it gets repaired." Nonsense. We heard the same arguments when external DVD drives became integrated into the PCs. PCs are super cheap and easy to build and repair. Personal laser printers are very reliable and are becoming more and more compact. Ans since workers will become more mobile and work-at-home types, it will become a natural solution — especially for college students. **Probability: 85%**

2. FOR A PERIOD OF A FEW YEARS, THERE WILL ONLY BE THREE MAJOR PRINTER AND COPIER/ MFP MANUFACTURERS. AFTER WHICH, THERE WILL EMERGE MANY AGILE SMALLER ONES

At some point in the next 6 to 8 years, the printer and copier/MFP market will experience an extreme level of consolidation, forced by a combination of bankruptcies, low margins, competition-elimination, and survival.

Low margins will force some providers to exit the business, and the shift in office output capacity will force the consolidation of others. The quest for profits in a lowered-margin business will provide licensing opportunities for small, agile tech-startups that will begin manufacturing and re-branding printers and MFPs to moderate success. **Probability: 70%**

3. THE PRICE OF MFPs WILL DROP SHARPLY AS THE PERCENTAGE OF FLATBED COPY DEVICES SHIPPED WITH 11" x 17" (A3) FORMAT DROPS TO BELOW 10% OF TOTAL UNITS

Anyone who performs office output assessments and captures detailed paper-usage metrics can see this one coming. In the next 3 to 4 years, manufacturers will cut production of A3 format MFPs dramatically, as companies simply stop buying them.

My study results show that, on average, about 9% of the total pages produced on MFPs in the general office (excluding production devices in the

Central Reprographics Department) are 11" x 17" format. Companies are slowly beginning to acknowledge the fact that users simply don't produce very many A3-sized documents anymore. Of course, there are some die-hards who refuse to believe that *every* user doesn't need 11" x 17" output capability, and will continue to purchase them in quantity. But they, too, will use data about their offices to make informed decisions, and will eventually change their purchase habits. **Probability: 90%**

4. APPLE COMPUTER WILL LAUNCH A NEW LINE OF STYLISH, PORTABLE COLOR PRINTERS THAT WILL DO FOR PRINTERS WHAT THE CANDY-COLORED iMAC DID FOR PCs

In the next 7 years, Apple, Inc. will get into the printer business as they look for new revenue streams in the hardware segment to make up for the revenue lost due to the maturity of the iPod and the iPhone (or whatever it will be called at the time of this printing).

Why *printers*, you ask? Because of licensing opportunities I described in a previous paragraph. I predicted that it will be a Wild West for agile printer manufacturers in several years, and Apple will be among them. Whether it's simply through a licensing arrangement or through some deeper level of alliance with a major printer manufacturer, Apple will enter the game and add style to the ho-hum printer designs of today. **Probability: 60%**

5. INK AND TONER COUNTERFEITING WILL GROW SO LARGE THAT A WELL-KNOWN PRINTER/ MFP MANUFACTURER WILL NOT BE ABLE TO OVERCOME THE LOSSES AND WILL SHUT ITS DOORS

It is estimated that, today, 10% to 12% of all printer/copier ink and toner sold is counterfeit. U.S. law defines counterfeiting as those items sold under a product name without proper authorization, where the identity of the source of the goods is knowingly and intentionally mislabeled in a way that suggests that it is the authentic, approved product.

In 10 years, not only will the losses force manufacturers to become more concerned about the growing threat of counterfeiting, but the cost that will be required just to combat counterfeiting will become so prohibitive to some manufacturers, that their survival will be held in the balance. **Probability: 65%**

6. DIGITAL WORKFLOW SOLUTIONS SUCH AS ENTERPRISE CONTENT MANAGEMENT WILL NOT GAIN WIDESPREAD ACCEPTANCE QUICKLY AND THE PRECENTAGE OF OFFICES WITH INEFFICIENT OUTPUT INFRASTRUCTURES WILL LEVEL-OUT AND REMAIN ABOUT THE SAME AS IT IS TODAY

Content and document management solutions hold great promise for reducing the amount of paper produced and wasted in offices around the world. The problem is that these solutions are complex to implement correctly and can be costly — with negligible financial ROI. In addition, 1/3 of all ECM systems fail within 2 years! the result has been slower-than-hoped-for widespread adoption of ECM solutions in the workplace.

In 5 years, I believe that, on average, the overall levels of corporate (in)efficiency will still be at the levels they are today. Regulatory compliance will not be reason enough to motivate companies to adopt ECM solutions company-wide. And with the growth in printer shipments going strong, and a leveling-out of corporate downsizing (and baby boomer retirements), the percentage of paper output growth will stabilize — forcing yet additional printer and MFP purchases — and erode any efficiency gains made in the past few years. **Probability 90%**

7. WITHIN THE NEXT 5 YEARS, 65% OF ALL CORPORATIONS WILL HAVE OUTSOURCED (SOME PORTION OF) THEIR OFFICE OUTPUT ENVIRONMENT

There is a budding trend in mid-size companies to eliminate their official IT departments and, instead, opt to hire young tech-savvy employees to fill the niche. Bold, huh? But a similar logic seems to be permeating the office output environments of major corporations. Many companies are turning over the reins to 3rd parties, and are removing themselves from the "tedious" job of ordering, administering, supporting, fixing and supplying printers, copiers, fax machines, supplies and consumables to their users.

In addition to relieving themselves of the "headaches," companies are also finding that it's an attractive financial proposition, too. **Probability: 85%**

8. PRINTERS, COPIERS, AND FAX MACHINES WILL BE CONFIGURED AND PROCURED DIRECTLY BY THE CORPORATION FROM THE MANUFACTURER'S WEBSITE AND/OR 1-800 NUMBER

In 5 years, the majority of company will have entered into outsourcing arrangements with 3rd parties to manage their office output environments. New acquisitions will be predominantly handled by the outsourcer, and any ancillary requirements will be filled on-line or by phone.

The direct procurement model has proven to be effective for ordering PCs, and the same will be true for printers and copiers/MFPs. Manufacturers will look to streamline distribution channels and reduce costs, while highly-knowledgeable customers will want the ability to do everything themselves: configure and order the devices; apply for corporate discounts; and buy flexible support packages. Many large corporations already do this with Intranet portals linked directly to their suppliers, so I believe it's only a matter of time until the majority of purchases are handled this way, too. **Probability: 75%**

9. AS HARDCOPY DEVICES BECOME MORE RELIABLE, AN INNOVATIVE COMPANY WILL BEGIN TO OFFER FLEXIBLE HARDCOPY SUPPORT PLANS AND REFUNDS FOR ANY UN-USED SUPPORT "DEPOSITS"

As hardcopy devices become more commoditized (less device differentiation), companies will gain a competitive advantage by providing better, more creative levels of service. Some innovative company will begin to offer service and support with up-front deposit payments that are totally refundable.

It will work something like this: Within 3 years, *Corporation A* will buy equipment and support from a hardware manufacturer. The manufacturer will bill the company up-front for the cost of an annual service agreement — for simplicity, let's say, $10,000.

Each time the service provider has to take a service call or go on-site to repair a device, the manufacturer will deduct the cost for the service call/visit — plus T&L — from the $10,000 service deposit. We'll assume the cost of this call was $2,000. So, in effect, the company has an $8,000 remaining service balance. If the manufacturer didn't have to take any more service calls from the company for the rest of the year, then the manufacturer will reimburse (or give a credit to) the company in the amount of the remaining balance — $8,000 — less the cost of capital and a few other charges. [Some service provider is going to read this book and use this idea, so I'll say the Probability is 100%]

10. NONE OF MY PROGNOSTICATIONS WILL COME TO FRUITION

Probability: 25%

AS I SPEAK WITH MANAGERS REGARDING OFFICE OUTPUT, I AM FREQUENTLY ASKED THE QUESTION, "HOW LONG SHOULD WE KEEP OUR PRINTERS AND COPIERS?" OR "WHY DO WE SIGN 5-YEAR LEASES FOR PRINTERS AND UP TO 7-YEAR LEASES FOR COPIERS/MFPs?" or similar questions about the "useful life" of these assets. Obviously, there is no single answer to such questions, and my first reply is often: It depends.

There is some rationale for the term companies sign technology equipment leases for — typically 3-to-5 years. There are also reasons why companies hold onto these assets for the amount of time they ultimately keep them; fundamentally, it has to do with the expected "useful life" of the assets.

According to Generally Accepted Accounting Principles (GAAP) the useful life for capital assets (i.e. computers and technology excluding software) is defined at 3-7 years. Corporations can amortize (depreciation, depletion, write off asset investments over the projected life of the assets) such assets over this time period. Typically, companies depreciate assets over either 3-years (technology is moving here), 4, or 5-years based on the number of years the company expects the asset to last or the amount of production they expect from an asset — *the useful life*. But either way, they are bound by the rules of GAAP and can't go beyond 7-years on their books. And since most technology is still purchased, companies follow these guidelines.

GAAP also says that you can't depreciate an asset for a term SHORTER than they determine to be an asset's minimal useful life. They believe that most computer assets have a minimum useful life of 3-years. That's one reason why you don't see companies depreciating computer assets for less than 3-years. Capitalization, yes. Depreciation, no.

One of the latest trends in the industry is how companies are being encouraged by consultants and manufacturers to *not* enter into copier/MFP agreements longer than 3-years. There are lots of reasons for this, but its primarily due to the fact that technology is rapidly changing and improving (becoming cheaper and more feature-rich), and being locked into long-term copier/MFP contracts will prohibit the company from taking advantage of more reliable, more efficient, more robust, less costly technology.

Many traditional copier manufacturers with lots of old analog eet will place these old, refurbished devices at companies under leases because the can do so at a low cost since the asset to the manufacturer is fully depreciated (no cost). The problem is that these devices are notoriously poor performers leading to many support and help desk calls (even though they may have a separate copier repair number to call) and to very dissatisfied and unproductive users.

Another reason why companies will hold onto a technology asset for the amount of time they do is because — after a certain period — the asset no longer provides a financial benefit to them (commonly 3-to-5 years of depreciation), and then they will replace it (no doubt after hearing from a sales rep how "new" replacement technology can help the company achieve its financial objectives). Remember the Investment Tax Credit? Some companies were refreshing hardware every year!

Consulting firms and manufacturers have found that "Higher costs result from aged devices 5+ years." They cite higher maintenance/parts, supplies, and toner costs; higher IT support costs because the devices are less network-manageable; and lower employee productivity because the devices lack advanced features/functions. In other words, aging printers/copiers/MFPs simply cost more to operate.

Workgroup printers that are more than 5 or 10-years old often have supplies costs of more than double the supplies costs of today's workgroup printers and MFPs. Some of the older printers don't even have the basic power management, so they are powered-on constantly, wasting electricity. The devices are also less reliable and contribute to user dissatisfaction. The result: PERSONAL PRINTERS start to show up everywhere!

Regarding the question of why leases are typically written for between 3-and-5 years, most leasing companies and financial institutions will only underwrite a computer asset for a term that they consider to be the asset's *useful life* – and that's typically 3-to-5 years for technology equipment. And as for utility-based pricing, such managed output arrangements are basically embedded leases, so you will invariably see typical terms of 3-to-5 year as well.

So, how long should you keep your printers, copiers, and MFPs? I say you should keep them as long as they meet the following criteria:

- They are within their depreciable-life — based on your accounting criteria
- They are operationally reliable and produce high-quality output (subjective, I know)
- Users do not lose productivity because of their use of the devices
- They have the user-demanded features and functions (e.g. color, finishing, scan-to)
- They are 7-years or older
- They have a Total Cost of Ownership comparable to new devices

And if your existing eet of devices doesn't meet the aforementioned criteria, then it's probably a good time consider an upgrade.

chapter sixteen
OUTRO

THERE ARE THREE SWITCHES IN A HALLWAY. One switch controls a light fixture in a room at the far end of the hall. The door to the room is closed, and you can't see whether the light is on or off. You need to find out which of the three switches controls the light. How can you find out the correct switch, making only one trip to the room?

[The solution is provided after the next page]

SOLUTION: Label the light switches 1, 2, and 3. Turn on switch #1 (and leave the other two switches turned off). Wait about 5 minutes, then turn switch #1 off and switch #2 on. Go to the room.

If the light is on when you get to the room, then you know that switch #2 is the correct switch. If the light is off but the bulb is *hot*, then you know the correct switch is switch #1. If the light is off and the bulb is cold, then the correct switch is number 3.

ABOUT THE AUTHOR

TAB EDWARDS is a consultant and author with over 23-years of experience in consulting, technology, sales & marketing, entrepreneurship and business management. Mr. Edwards earned his undergraduate degree from the University of Pittsburgh, and his MBA degree from the Pennsylvania State University.

He began his business journey at the tender age of 13, selling inexpensive household items door-to-door. Although he has held award-winning sales, consulting and management positions at some of the words most admired companies — including IBM Corporation, General Electric, the Sales & Marketing Consulting Company (SMCC), Gimbel Brothers, and Hewlett-Packard Company — he cites his door-to-door encyclopedia salesman job at Collier's Encyclopedia as the job that taught him some of the most valuable lessons about business.

Mr. Edwards shares his breadth of knowledge and experience by working with a broad range of companies including non-profit agencies, small & medium businesses, and *Fortune 500* Corporations.

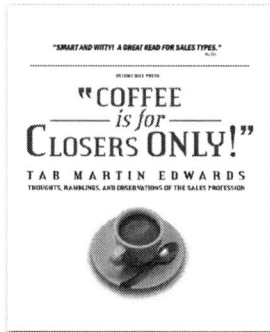